VISIONS
OF
COURAGE
THE BOBBY SMITH STORY

BOBBY E. SMITH Ph.D.

Copyright 1998
Bobby Smith
Revised Reprint 2000
2nd Revised Reprint 2002
3rd Revised Reprint 2005
4th Revised Reprint 2006
5th Revised Reprint 2008
6th Revised Reprint 2009

ISBN# 1-885857-22-3

VOC Publishing
120 North Fair Street
Marksville, Louisiana 71351
(318) 240-8209
bobbysmith@visionsofcourage.com
www.visionsofcourage.com

Printed in the United States of America by:
Litho Printers & Bindery
Cassville, MO 65625

*"In loving memory of our precious daughter,
Kimberley Denyce Smith."*

August 2, 1975 - September 29, 1997

ACKNOWLEDGEMENTS

There are so many people I would like to thank for their contributions to this book and in my life personally; but, time and space do not allow for me to thank each one individually, so for those of you I do not mention in this section, it's not because I am ungrateful. I am thankful to each of you for your prayers, support and guidance throughout the course of my life.

First, I would like to thank God, without whom I could not go on. I would like to thank my dad first and foremost for instilling in me the importance of never giving up. Thanks to Danny, my older brother, who has always been the family protector and defender. Terry, thanks for being a leader and for teaching me to be a leader and not a follower. My heartfelt thanks goes to my twin sister, Betty, who hurt emotionally more than I did, during the hard times. Unless you are a twin, you could not understand the closeness of our relationship. Thanks to Kevin, my younger brother, who chauffeured me and my blind school buddies. Thanks to all of my family and friends inside and outside of law enforcement. Each of you have made such a wonderful difference in my life. Special thanks to Carol Glover Mathus for her countless hours of transcription and her enduring friendship. Thanks to Nicole Hoppel whose editing polished this manuscript to completion.

Finally, a very special thanks to my loving wife Janie. If it had not been for her support and gentle prodding throughout the years, I would have never written, much less completed, this project. Thanks to my two children, Kim and Brad, who have been the joy of my life. Although I've never seen Brad, I've been told that he looks just like I spit him out of my mouth. I can only hope that I can pass on the integrity, strong moral values and character that I've learned from my family & friends. God bless and keep each of you.

The Master's Bouquet
By Christi Robinson

Today I had a vision of heaven in my mind, I saw fields of flowers, of every different kind.

There were violets and lilies far as the eye could see, but to my surprise (and my dismay) they didn't notice me.

Their gaze was fixed upon a light that shone so brilliantly, I strove to see from whence it came, but its glory blinded me.

And then I heard a melody, so sweet upon my ear. The flowers sang so beautifully as if the light could hear!

The moments passed and as I watched my eyes adjusted some – and suddenly I realized into whose presence I had come.

The Beautiful Rose of Sharon sat in the midst of them, and all these heavenly flowers were the saints adoring Him!

And then my gaze was shifted to a soft and tender sight. The servant-blossoms presented their King with a precious gift – sealed tight.

And as the seal was broken, a glow escaped within. The tiny gift revealed itself and then I noticed them –

A tiny cluster of rosebuds arranged in a beautiful way, it was then I saw my baby, in the midst of the Master's Bouquet.

I feared she would not know me, and then her eyes met mine. Her rosy cheeks and soft, pink skin said, "Mom, I'm doing fine."

She said, "I'm happy here in heaven worshipping my King," then with all the other rosebuds she began to softly sing.

The bouquet sang all together; their music filled the air, sweet praises to their Maker that only they could share.

Then my child looked at me and smiled 'til I thought my heart would burst. She said, "I love you, Mommy, but Jesus loved me first."

Then I saw my little Terri in a new and glorious way. "Twas for this she was created - to be a bud in the Master's Bouquet.

She quickly threw me a sheepish grin - it was clear she was very fond of Him - And all her other rosebud friends joined in, as they began to sing again:

"Holy, Holy, Holy, Lord God Almighty!
Our Creator, Our Redeemer
The Lord giveth and the Lord taketh away.
Blessed be the name of the Lord."

TABLE OF CONTENTS

FOREWORD

First Sergeant Gary Aschenbach
Maryland State Police

Guest speakers truly are similar to ships in the night. Many times we make presentations without knowing who we precede or who we follow. That is how Bobby Smith and I first came to meet in Biloxi, Mississippi. Having heard his name on numerous occasions, he came strongly recommended as one of those dynamic speakers not to be missed. So needless to say, I found myself in the company of 500 other police officers as we carefully listened and evaluated our own lives in comparison to that of the Bobby Smith story.

You see, as a sworn Trooper in the State of Louisiana, Bobby was critically wounded while performing a "routine" traffic stop on March 14, 1986. As he voluntarily responded to stop a motorist who had purposely maneuvered around a driver's license check point, his life was destined to be changed forever. Changed as a result of a simple traffic stop similar to those he had "routinely" performed hundreds of times prior as an eleven-year veteran officer. This stop, however, was unlike any he had ever experienced.

As he approached the vehicle, which was hidden under the cover of darkness, he came face to face with a 12 gauge shotgun in the hands of a crazed killer. At a mere distance of twenty-nine feet, he witnessed what turned out to be his last sight forever. Two blasts of pellets from the No. 5 load rounds threatened his every heartbeat. Though he had somehow miraculously survived both shots, the second of the two resulted in his complete and total blindness from that night forward.

After years of physical and intense mental recovery, Bobby is committed to giving international presentations to police officers with the unselfish hopes of preventing similar tragedies to others. His talks are not given with the intent to gain popularity or sympathy. Nor are they presented in a chastising manner towards himself or others. Instead, his approach is of such that he teaches us not only how to avoid falling victim to a similar situation but how to deal with the aftershock of traumatic situations in our own lives.

His unique introduction began that day with his relentless humor of walking through a K-Mart department store and accidentally knocking inventory onto the floor with his white cane . . . the same cane, incidentally, that he was later chastised for painting "police" blue. It was this and other nonconforming type behavior that contributed to his eventual dismissal from his short-lived experience in "Blind School." As he humorously compared the school to the movie "One Flew Over the Cuckoo's Nest," he admitted that the real reason he deliberately dropped out of the school was to negate being certifiably blind. Police officers can appreciate that. If you're not "certified," then it just can't be so!

As his presentation continued, the true meaning became overwhelmingly obvious to us all. His message was clear and simple; stay safe and remain unscrupulously loyal to yourself, your family, and your work, in that order. Before long, the grades were in and the horrific impact he made on all of us was evidenced by the hundreds of sniffles, tear wiping, and deliberate coughs used to disguise our true feelings.

These genuine emotions were not offered or prompted as a kind gesture of pity or sympathy for Bobby or his unfortunate injury. On the contrary, they were a result of recognizing our own shortcomings and injustices to which we had subjected ourselves and families over the years of our careers. He painfully, yet tactfully, brought to light how we too often inappropriately prioritize those things which are, or should be, important to our lives. In my twenty-five years as a Trooper and instructor, I have never seen an assembly of seasoned officers outwardly respond and be so emotionally touched as I had witnessed that day.

It was several months later that Bobby and I again had the opportunity to meet, as he had agreed to make a presentation in Maryland. Of course, his visit didn't come without its own vice. I was unaware that because he accepted an invitation to stay at our home, that we would be obligated to make certain concessions in an attempt to avoid offending his Southern sensitivities. So my wife agreed to cook for him, in the middle of the night, something called "ras-n-aggs" (rice and eggs). First, he had to interpret what exactly was "ras-n-aggs." On top of that, he wanted something with it called "grits." While we did make the rice and eggs, we just laughed at the very suggestion of some grits. His only comment, made in a disappointed voice, was, "Oh, well, I must be too far north, and these Yankees don't know any better." In retrospect, I have to admit that it was pretty good, but we haven't treated ourselves to "ras-n-aggs" since.

The timing of his visit was sad but unfortunately, very appropriate. We had just lost two Maryland State Troopers in the line of duty. Within two months, one was killed on a traffic stop and the other in a motor vehicle accident while responding to back-up another police officer. Bobby did more than "walk his talk" that night. Prior to his intense, four-hour presentation, he met privately with the families of the fallen heroes in an attempt to console them. I returned shortly thereafter only to find them quietly holding and comforting each other in a short prayer.

Like the changing of the guard, Bobby stood in front of 350 police officers and other friends and family of the slain Troopers as if he had known them his entire life. Within minutes, the crowd was uncontrollably laughing at jokes targeting his own disability. However, the laughing was soon turned to somber tears as he recounted the story of the fatal mistakes he made on the evening of his shooting. He warned us not to repeat his same tactical errors, and he related to us the time he offered to help his son assemble a McDonald's toy. With no malicious intent, Brad said, "Thanks, dad, but how can you help me? Your eyes are broken."

As Bobby defined the acronym spelled by the B.A.D.G.E displayed proudly on each of our uniforms, he painfully reminded us to identify and prioritize those things in our own lives that are, and should be, important. At the conclusion of his presentations, he offered a challenge to us all - to return home to our families that evening, turn off our pagers, disconnect the telephone, and take a minute to wrestle around on the floor with our children. While not necessarily a unique idea, it's one that had been forgotten for far too long. And as the music to "You Are My Hero" had already begun to play in the background, he continued with that challenge for us to make the best use of the quality time God has given us, and to do so in a way that we can forever stand proud.

As he climbed the stairs to the rear of the amphitheater, he was greeted with a line of handshakes, hugs and tears. As I stood back and watched the emotions flow, I realized that it was as if he had somehow purposely lost his eyesight, so that he could teach us how to see.

It's not often that we receive the rare opportunity to

participate in a truly memorable occasion during the course of our lives. It is my honor to have been invited to introduce and pay tribute to a genuine friend and hero who, without reservation, shares with us his tragic life encounters in an effort to benefit us. Bobby Smith is an authentic hero who has not only fallen; but, through his personal determination and help from his family and friends, has successfully triumphed over his own adversities.

As I recall his life story, two questions continue to haunt me. How would I have faired under similar conditions, and how can I utilize one person's tragedy to better myself? Bobby's recovery was certainly not accomplished without sacrifices. He lost his family, career, financial stability and worse, the priceless loss of his eyesight. When I asked about the relentless hatred he must feel towards his assailant, I was surprised to learn that he does not hold any animosity. Instead, he believes that never-ending hatred is akin to a slow death, allowing more of one's life to be stolen every day. Bobby Smith is definitely about *life* and not *death*!

I invite you to avoid the inevitable blindness of our lives, by seeing through the eyes of Bobby Smith.

> Good luck and God bless!
> Your admiring friend,
> Gary

"TFC BOBBY E. SMITH"

CHAPTER 1
THE SHOOTING

I radioed in to the Winnsboro Sheriff's office, "F-18 to Winnsboro, I'll be following a small reddish vehicle north on LA 15 approximately at mile post 99."

I was traveling approximately 85 to 90 miles per hour trying to catch up with the small reddish vehicle as it sped through the driver's license check point that the State Police and the Franklin Parish Sheriff's Department had set up three miles south of Winnsboro on LA 15. As I got closer to the vehicle, I observed the driver reach toward the passenger's side - reaching as if trying to pick up something. I then observed him reach underneath the seat as he bent forward. My thoughts rushed back to just the week before, when on this same highway I was in a chase much the same as this one. On this particular chase, the car came to an abrupt stop and the driver jumped from his car and started running across the field. I jumped from my car and raced after him, caught him and placed him under arrest. That wasn't going to happen again. I wasn't going to get my uniform dirty chasing some punk across that field. I was ready for him.

By this time I was within five or six car lengths from the vehicle. Suddenly, he slammed on his brakes. I was traveling at a much faster rate of speed than the suspect. I knew that hitting my brakes would not be enough to keep me from hitting the vehicle in the rear end, so I swerved to the left into the inside northbound lane. As I went past the vehicle, I noticed the driver's door was opening, but at that time, I saw no one exiting the vehicle.

It was 11:30 p.m. on a Friday night. There was total darkness around us as there were no street lights on the state highway just south of town. Then, in my mind, I began to process my training as a 10-year police veteran. Go on up, turn your vehicle around, get on the opposite shoulder of the road, place your spotlight on the vehicle, and locate the suspect before you exit the vehicle. I remember making these conscious thoughts, but to no avail I was influenced by a personality that most police officers have, which is the competitive spirit. We want to catch the prey, retrieve the quarry, make the apprehension at whatever cost - even if it would mean compromising our personal safety.

I quickly pulled my vehicle in front of the violator's vehicle, placing my car two or three car lengths just north of his front bumper. I immediately opened the door, stepped from my unit and headed toward the violator's vehicle. At this point, I realized that I had made a serious tactical error. As I turned around at a slow trot looking toward the violator's vehicle, the first thing I realized was the headlights of the suspect's vehicle were in my eyes. I was blinded by the light. I began to move toward the shoulder of the road in an effort to get out of the headlights. I remember the helpless feeling that overcame me, like I was a duck in a shooting gallery. In an effort to try to correct the mistake that I had made, I left myself wide open in the middle of the street with no cover. I began to move away from the suspect's vehicle toward the west side of the highway to try to get my focus off of the headlights and onto the suspect. I pulled my revolver, a Smith & Wesson Model 66 .357 magnum, and shouted a command for the violator to place his hands on the hood of his car. A shotgun blast rang off; I remember seeing the fire from the shotgun barrel, looking like fifty roman candles tied together, shoot out fifteen to twenty feet from the suspect's shotgun. I was on the ground, but didn't remember how I got there. "Had I been hit?" I wondered. "Had I fallen? Had I just stumbled?" I wasn't sure.

I fired one shot toward the gunshot blast that I had seen, not knowing if my shot would hit the target. Simultaneously, as my bullet was traveling through the air, the suspect fired a second round. This time I was an easier target, lying totally still 29 feet away from him. This time his aim was perfect. The shotgun blast hit me directly in the face. I felt no pain, but instantly, my sight was gone. I remember seeing stars as they began to flash inside my head. Lots of confusion. Had I hit the suspect? Was he going to shoot me again? Was I going to die? All of these thoughts began to pass through my mind as I lay there face down on the highway with blood running down my face.

VISIONS OF COURAGE

CHAPTER 2
THE DAY OF THE SHOOTING

The alarm on my clock went off at 6:30 a.m. on Friday morning March 14, 1986. I got out of bed and started with my daily routines just as on any ordinary day. I sat on the couch drinking a cup of coffee as I watched the morning news, thinking of the day's events ahead. Although I didn't have to report to work until 2 p.m., my morning was full of things that had to be done. A good friend of mine had leased me 100 acres, and it was time to disc the fields to prepare for a new crop. So I got myself ready and headed to the land that was about ten or twelve miles from my house.

When I got to the field, I climbed upon my John Deere tractor and looked across the land. I enjoyed farming, mainly because I didn't have to make a living from it. Farming was a time of relaxation for me, and it was also a time to release some of the stress of being a Louisiana State Trooper. As I began to disc, the field worms and insects were uncovered, which left them open prey for the birds that flew above. The further I went with my plowing, I noticed a small rabbit in the field. As I made each round in the field, the unplowed area, which served as cover for the small animals, became smaller and smaller. Each time I made a pass around the field, the rabbit would move to the unplowed area. All of a sudden I noticed a hawk perched upon a high line above the field, waiting for the appropriate time to swoop down on his prey. Then the inevitable finally came. I made my last pass through the field, leaving nothing but freshly plowed ground. The rabbit's cover from his prey had been taken

5

away. I stopped my tractor as I saw the hawk finally leave his perch. The rabbit raced across the open field trying desperately to reach more cover that was now 100 yards away, but his effort was to no avail. The hawk swooped down on the small animal and pinned him to the ground with his powerful talons. I sat there and watched the hawk devour his prey. I was astonished at how tragic "survival of the fittest" was, being totally unaware of the fact that in just twelve short hours, I too, would be personally involved in a battle for survival of the fittest.

I climbed into my truck and headed to the house to clean up and get a workout before I had to report to work. When I arrived at the house, Sammy was there waiting for me. Sammy was not only my best friend; he was my workout partner as well. He was already dressed in his workout clothes and tennis shoes, (untied as usual), ready to go to the gym. He was a big guy, 6 ft. 2 in. with 220 pounds of pure muscle. Sammy's body frame looked as though he was a competitive weight lifter. However, his muscles were formed on the farm and not in a gym. His eyes always sparkled like a mischievous little boy. As my truck came to a stop at the house, I got out.

Sammy called out to me, "What took you so long, sissy? Let's go get a workout!"

I changed clothes, and we drove to the gym we owned. When we got there, we decided that we would move some of the equipment into the parking lot, because it was such a beautiful day. We worked out about an hour and a half, and I realized that my time was running short. I needed to go home to get ready to report to work at 2 p.m. After our workout was over, I drove back home to clean up and get ready for work.

As I unlocked the door to the house, I could hear

the phone ringing. I stepped in the door and answered the phone. It was Waldo, the radio operator for the Tensas Parish Sheriff's Department.

"Hey, Bobby, Lt. McDonald just called and said as soon as you get in to call him at the Franklin Parish Sheriff's Department."

I told Waldo to call him back and let him know that as soon as I showered and got ready for work I would give him a call. I jumped in the shower and began getting ready. I opened the closet to retrieve the thing that I had worked so hard for - my Louisiana State Police uniform. I felt proud every day that I put that uniform on. I pulled the shirt off the hanger and put it on. I admired myself in the mirror as I buttoned up my shirt, feeling so proud. Then I placed my Coreno gun belt on and headed to my State Police unit, F-18, ready to start my shift. I slid into my seat, cranked my unit, and notified St. Joe that I was in service.

As I made the drive to St. Joseph, Louisiana, the county seat of Tensas Parish, I listened to Jimmy Buffet singing "Wasting Away in Margaritaville".

When I drove up to the Tensas Parish Sheriff's Department, Waldo was there working the radio room. He waved for me to come in and have a cup of coffee. I walked in and spoke to Waldo, who had already started fixing me a cup of coffee.

"Same as always, Smith, one Sweet & Low and a touch of cream," Waldo said as I walked in.

Waldo was the radio operator that was assigned to my shift. I would always tease him about starting to workout with Sammy and I, because Waldo was a little overweight. I told him that Sammy and I could make him a lean, mean fighting machine. As usual, Waldo would just smile, decline my offer, and reach in his pocket and pull out another Winston.

Waldo got Lt. McDonald on the phone while I kicked back in his chair and rested my feet on his desk. Before handing me the phone he said, "Get your feet off my desk. You think you own this place or something?" He smiled as he always did and handed me the phone.

Lt. McDonald informed me that we would be conducting a driver's license check that evening in Winnsboro. He went on to say that several deputies from the local Sheriff's Department and some of the troopers would be joining us. We were just going out to do a little public relations. We decided to meet around 6 p.m. for dinner and to get our orders for the evening.

As I hung up the phone, I turned to Waldo, "Well, I better go do a little enforcement in your parish before I have to meet the lieutenant tonight. See you later, Waldo." I never realized how much we took those three little words for granted. I had no idea that after that night I would never see Waldo again.

I went to my unit and drove back by the gym where Sammy was finishing his workout in order to let him know that I would be working in Winnsboro that night and not Tensas Parish. After talking with Sammy, I headed towards Winnsboro, making a few traffic stops on the way. When I got to the Franklin Parish Sheriff's Office, I saw Trooper Shelly Brown, who was the resident trooper for Winnsboro. We greeted each other and started into the Sheriff's Office. Once inside, we met Deputy Larry Crum, the K-9 deputy, who offered us a fresh cup of coffee. Deputy Crum's black lab followed us down the hall to the coffee room, just as if he were a fellow officer. As we sat there drinking our coffee, Deputy Don McDuffie and Lt. Don McDonald arrived, and we began discussing what we would be doing that night.

Once again Lt. McDonald informed us that we would just be doing a little public relations. We were to make sure the people had up-to-date licenses, registration, and insurance.

After our briefing, we got in our units and headed south on LA 15. We stationed our units about five miles south of Winnsboro. LA 15 was a four-lane highway, two lanes headed north and two lanes headed south, separated by a grassy median. We positioned ourselves in the northbound lanes and proceeded to stop the oncoming traffic. After working the traffic for about two hours and giving a few citations, we decided to break for dinner.

VISIONS OF COURAGE

CHAPTER 3
THE SURVIVAL

Lying face down on the center lane of the highway I could feel the blood running down my face, but I felt no pain. I wondered to myself, "Will this be the day that you die?" I had no idea where the suspect was hiding. I heard a vehicle door slam. Next, I heard six shots then an additional shot. I wondered, "Are these shots hitting me? Is the suspect continuing to shoot me? Is this my backup coming to help me out? Where are these shots coming from?"

With the only defensive move I could muster, I began to remove myself from the present reality. I began to mentally fade from the brutish nightmare that had overtaken my life and from the conscious present to my subconscious past.

I began remembering the training that I had received at the Louisiana State Police Training Academy. I could hear Aubrey Futrell talking in my mind. He was our defensive tactics and officer survival trainer. He played offensive guard on the Louisiana Tech football team during the late 60's. You may not recognize the name Aubrey Futrell, but you would probably recognize the name of the quarterback that he protected in the backfield: Terry Bradshaw. Like Bradshaw, Aubrey was also a fierce competitor and a very strong athlete. I wondered what Aubrey would think of me if I gave up. I recalled Aubrey telling us that if we were ever in a traumatic event, it's important for us to stay conscious. Think survival; think that you will live, and you will. I remembered his saying, "Bang! Bang! doesn't mean you're dead;

it means shots have been fired." I focused on that thought. *As a child we played cops and robbers, calling out "Bang! Bang! You're dead!"* Those words became detrimental. Does *"Bang! Bang!"* really mean you're dead? Does it mean only that shots have been fired? I was confused. I felt no pain, but could literally feel my life's force running down my face. I continued to focus on that mental process — you can live if you choose to live, and you don't give up. As I lay there in the middle of the highway, I recalled a story Aubrey told us of an officer who was shot through the right arm, only a flesh wound, but because he truly believed in the saying *"Bang! Bang! You're dead!"* he lay there and died. Thoughts of survival began to run through my head. I began audibly reciting my name, social security number, driver's license number, address, unit number, birth dates and any number I could think of to try and keep myself from going into shock. "Was I still conscious? Could I hear myself talking?" Yes, I was still conscious and yes, I could hear myself, so I must still be alive.

Things quickly became very frantic at the scene. I could hear cars driving up, car doors slamming and people yelling. The voices around me began shouting commands. "Someone get an ambulance!" "Is Bobby okay?" "Someone watch and make sure no one runs over him lying there in the middle of the blacktop!" I could hear the excitement and fear in each officer's voice. In the midst of the confusion, I heard a man run toward me. He knelt down and placed his hands upon my shoulder and rolled me over. After he saw my face, he screamed, *"Oh my God!"* and ran off. I could only imagine the horrible sight that he must have seen. My face was full of blood and holes where the pellets had entered my face and forehead. My left eyeball had been shot from the socket and was partially lying on my cheek. The top of my scalp had been ripped off where the shotgun pellets had ripped through my head.I must have looked extremely grotesque. The physical threat of the battle had concluded and now the tougher mental portion accelerated.

I began role-playing in my mind. Aubrey had taught us many times in class about role playing, and that in role playing you must play the game as if it was real. This time, I was no longer assuming that it were real. It was, much too real. You have to envision yourself surviving, see yourself walking away from a shooting — and you will.

I was an athlete, a competitive power lifter. Therefore, I related my survival to an athletic event. I remember while lying there on the highway, I saw in my mind a big, black scoreboard with bright yellow and red numbers. The light was lit up for the fourth quarter. I read the score. We were the visitors, and we were ahead by four points. The time remaining was :01. It was fourth down in the fourth quarter. I could see the home team lined up on the first yard line. Although I never played linebacker, there I was. Everyone knew what was going to happen. As the offensive team broke the huddle, they knew this would be their only play left in the game. If they scored, they would win. If they failed, they would lose. The offensive team came to the line, and there was a lone set back, the quarterback and fullback. At this time everything went into slow motion. I watched the quarterback from the left linebacker slot as the quarterback rang out his commands and snapped the ball. As the snap was made, the quarterback turned to his right, and there came the fullback ready to accept the ball. The quarterback laid the ball in the open arms of the fullback. The offensive line had made a hole for him in the defense. There I was, the linebacker filling that hole. I ducked my helmet and so did he, as we met there on the goal line. As we hit, I could

13

hear the groans of players around me. We both went to the ground. Had my tackle been a success? Had he scored? This was not just a game, it was life or death for me. If he scores, I lose; if he doesn't, I win; I would get a second chance at life. I came up from the tackle and looked to the sidelines. There was Aubrey Futrell with his hands in the air jumping and screaming with delight. I knew then that I had overcome death.

My thoughts rushed back to the State Police Academy. I remembered how Aubrey had pushed each of us beyond our physical, mental and emotional limits. The academy was a paramilitary organization, and our training was very much akin to the military's basic training programs. I recalled asking Aubrey, "Why do you put our class through so much — the push-ups, sit-ups and running?" He gave me that special, steely-eyed look and replied, "One day you will understand." This was that one-day. It all came into focus, and I truly understood the purpose of it all.

CHAPTER 4
IT WAS A SPECIAL DAY

It was December 12, 1962, a special day for my twin sister, Betty and me. Betty and I were in the fifth grade. During the school day, we would look at each other and smile, anticipating our special day. At 3:20 p.m., school was out. We grabbed our backpacks and rushed out to where the buses were lined up to take us home. We hurried up the steps of the bus and took our seat.

The bus ride home seemed to take forever. At each stop, children would unload, and we would go again. It seemed to last forever, and the excitement was mounting for our special day. Finally, the bus would come to a stop, and the doors would open. We would jump from our seats and run up the long driveway. As we got closer to the house, we noticed there were additional cars there than should have been on our special day. We ran around the cars to the back door into the kitchen. There were people standing around in the living room. Our eyes focused on the adults in the living room. Something was wrong. It took only a few seconds to realize everyone was somber. Some were crying. I thought to myself, *why is everyone crying? It's supposed to be a special day. Why is everyone crying?*

Aunt Irma walked over to us, with tears rolling down her face. Betty and I were standing there, staring at her with puzzled looks on our faces. Aunt Irma knelt down next to us. With tears streaming down her face, she hugged each one of us.

She said, "I am so sorry kids, your mother is dead."

15

December 12, 1962. The day our mother died was supposed to be a special day, the day of Betty's and my tenth birthday.

My mama, Alma, was one of 12 children who grew up in Jena, Louisiana. My mama was a wild child of the family. She was adventuresome, constantly seeking excitement. My mama had black hair, dark eyes, and an olive complexion. My daddy, Lavon Smith, one of five children, grew up in Pineville, Louisiana. He had brown hair, light complexion, and green eyes.

Opposites attract. This was surely the case of my mama and daddy. My mama was outgoing, a conversationalist. She loved to tell stories and always had a smile on her face. My dad was just the opposite. He was a very quiet, gentle man with a kind, humble spirit. My dad was very loving. Today we would call him an introvert.

My mom and dad met in high school. They dated for two years. It was 1945, following World War II. My daddy had been drafted and was stationed at Fort Polk, located in Leesville. Following boot camp, my mom and dad decided to get married. But they weren't telling anyone. My dad went to his sergeant and asked for a weekend leave to get married. The sergeant told my dad that he couldn't leave boot camp for the weekend and had to stay to stand guard. But dad was persistent and went to two of his comrades and told them of his plan to leave the base for the weekend to go to Pineville and marry my mother.

"Lavon," they asked, "didn't the sergeant tell you that you couldn't leave for the weekend?"

"Yes, that is what he said, but what he don't know won't hurt him."

My dad coaxed his two buddies to cover for him on guard duty, and my dad sneaked out and caught a bus to Pineville, some 40 miles away, to meet my mom. My dad was AWOL. I guess he was more adventuresome than we give him credit for. It was a Friday night when my dad arrived dressed in his army attire at Philadelphia Baptist Church, where the wedding was to be held. The day following the wedding, mom and dad were to report back to Fort Polk to spend their honeymoon. Even though he found out about my dad leaving without permission, my dad's sergeant must have been a little sentimental. I guess the sight of my dad and mom together softened his heart, and no disciplinary action was taken.

After their honeymoon at Fort Polk, Mom would go back and live in Pineville, and Dad was transferred to El Paso, Texas. For the next year and a half, their relationship was long distance. My mom would stay at home, and my dad would return as often as he could. In 1949, my dad returned to Pineville to be with my mom. One year later, they would have their first child, a son, my oldest brother, Danny.

Dad went to work for the VA hospital in Alexandria, Louisiana. My dad retired from the same institution 35 years later. My mom worked at Walgreen's. Two years after the birth of Danny, their second child, Terry was born. Papa and Grannie Smith lived in the Philadelphia community, some 15 miles east of Pineville. After Terry's birth, mom, dad, and their two kids would move next to my grandparents in a small house. There were no luxuries. Although we did have running water and indoor facilities, it was far from a mansion. Dispite being raised in what we would now consider a very poor environment, we didn't consider ourselves poor. Growing up was amazing. There was so much love in our house that we didn't realize there was not any money.

In 1952, two years after Terry's birth, mom and dad were told that they were expecting twins. On December 12,

1952, my twin sister, Betty, and I were born. But the joyous occasion would be short-lived.

Shortly after the birth, my mother began to have complications. She developed lesions and sores over her body, externally and internally. My mother was also diabetic, which only enhanced the disease. From the time of my birth to the time of her death in 1962, my mother lived in constant excruciating pain. I would see my mom crying, and I would climb in her lap to try and comfort her, although I needed comforting myself.

Although mom lived in excruciating pain, I never heard her complain. She always tried to maintain a smile on her face and put her best foot forward. She spent a lot of time in the hospital. She would be gone for weeks at a time. She was extremely ill, but I never knew this as a child, not by her actions or demeanor. I remember my mom being ill in bed, and we would climb up in bed with her. She loved to hear us sing. Mama loved southern gospel music. She always made sure we went to church every Sunday, and when we weren't in church, we would sit in the bed with mom and listen to her read the Bible to us. She was a great storyteller, using her voice and expressions, as she told us about Daniel in the lions' den and the most important story of all; the birth, life and death of Jesus Christ.

Mama's faith was very strong. She believed the only way to live was to have a close relationship with Jesus Christ, and she daily lived those convictions. My brothers, sister, and I followed their example of faith, and as children, we asked Jesus to come into our heart.

My dad worked full time at the hospital and also had a part time job at a cotton gin in Alexandria. My mama's illness was a financial strain on the family, and dad had to work extra to put food on the table. But I wouldn't trade my mom, dad or childhood for anyone else's.

I was seven years old, and sitting on the floor while my mom tied my new shoes. But they weren't new, just hand-me-down shoes.

I looked at my mom and said, "Mom, why can't I have new shoes like the other kids?"

My mom looked at me with sadness in her eyes and said, "We just can't afford new shoes, but I have cleaned and polished these shoes, and put new shoestrings in them. No one will ever know that they aren't new."

"I know, Mom. I was just wondering why I can't have shoes like the other kids." I was only seven years old, for heaven's sake. I didn't understand financial responsibilities. I just wanted a new pair of shoes like the other kids.

"But mom, shoes can't be that expensive. Why can't I have new shoes like the other kids?"

My mom, who lived in excruciating pain and who never experienced the finer things of life, was in the process of teaching me a very valuable lesson. A lesson I would recall for the rest of my life. My mama stood to her feet; I was sitting on the floor staring up at her. She reminded me of a soldier standing at attention with her hands down by her side and her head straight ahead. My mom began to speak in a bold, confident voice. Still staring straight ahead, she said, in a loud voice, "I complained because I had no shoes, until I saw the man who had no feet."

My mom relaxed her stature, sat down next to me and continued to lace up my shoes. My mom had taught me at the age of seven, a valuable lesson. A lesson I will never forget. Stop complaining about the things you don't have, but appreciate the things you do have.

The next three years, would be extremely difficult. My mom's condition would worsen. The doctors told my mom and dad that she wouldn't have long to live, but she never gave up on life. She never quit. My mama never fully learned how to ride a bike, but even up until her last day, she continued to try to learn. Danny and Terry, as I recall, would push her around the circle in front of our house. They would push, and she would pedal. She would say, "I think I've got it," and tell my brothers to let go. As they did, she would go a little distance and then topple over. This scene would be repeated time and time and time again. I have to give her credit. Although she never conquered that bicycle, she never stopped trying. Death and riding a bicycle are two things my mama never conquered, but today she is alive forever in heaven and riding her bike on the streets of gold.

My mama was just a country girl, and she loved to pick blackberries. Many years, she would come from the hospital when the blackberries would be in full bloom. We would go to the blackberry patch by Hooper Cemetery, located a few miles from our home. Our fingers and lips would be stained purple from eating the blackberries. And there was Mama in the middle of that blackberry patch, picking the berries with her dark hair pulled back into a ponytail and a purple stain around her lips. My mama would say that for everything great, there has to be a labor. We would soon forget the labor of picking those blackberries in the hot Louisiana sun as mom would pull a blackberry pie out of the oven and set it on the table. We would sit around the table waiting for the pie to cool down, so we could have a slice.

Although we qualified for the government welfare program, my dad never saw this as an option. My dad was a selfless man. He gave everything he had to his children. My dad was a man of honor, character, and integrity. If you want something in life, you have to work for it, he would say. There is no such thing as getting a free lunch. There are some people who are needy, who need the welfare program, he would say. But not those people who could work.

I remember early one evening when there was a knock on the door. My mom, dad, brothers and sister were sitting in the den. My dad got up to answer it, and it was an insurance salesman friend from high school. They exchanged greetings, and my dad invited the man aside. As they went to the kitchen table, the man began to tell my dad the importance of having insurance and saving for college for the kids. I sat there listening to the conversation between my dad and the man.

My dad said, " I don't know if my kids will go to college. That decision will be left up to them. But if they decide to go, they will pay their own way."

It wasn't that dad didn't believe in things being given to you. We grew up in that type of community where people helped those in need. Where I came from, everyone was in some form of need. Anything worth having was worth sacrificing for, dad believed. My dad knew about sacrifice, because he had grown up that way.

It was 1960. My mother's health deteriorated rapidly in the next two years. It seemed that mama stayed in the hospital more than she stayed at home, and she was greatly missed. We would visit her in the hospital, and it was difficult watching her in that bed. She always seemed to muster up enough energy to smile for us. We always had to sing her a song. That was her favorite thing.

It was the first weekend in December in 1962 that we visited our mom for the last time. We knew, even as children, that she wouldn't last much longer. We would sing her a song as usual and give her a hug and kiss. It must have been extremely difficult for our mom to smile at us with tears rolling down her face, knowing she would never see us again.

Not in this life, anyway. Doctors told my dad to go home and prepare for her funeral. My mom was a very determined lady, and her faith in God was strong. She told my dad that there was no need to prepare her funeral tomorrow that she would not die until she saw her babies' birthday, December 12, 1962.

Betty and I stood there in shock as Aunt Irma continued hugging our necks. My dad went to the funeral home to pick out a casket. We met Danny and Terry and drove to town to meet dad. We walked in with our dad, who walked over to look at the caskets. The lid was open. My mother was white. I'm sure we didn't understand the impact of the death. We were only children.

Danny, Terry, Betty and I were sitting on the steps of the funeral home. Continental Trailway was down the street, and we watched the people load and unload as the buses pulled off. Where were these buses coming from? Where were they going? I wish I was on one of those buses. I wish I could run away. Anywhere from here, anywhere but here. But running away wouldn't bring back my mama. We were seated on the front row of Philadelphia Baptist Church, where fifteen years earlier my mom and dad had stood in the same spot as they traded vows, to have and to hold, til death do us part. Unfortunately, that time had come. I sat next to Betty and held her hand. Betty was used to being the one who held MY hand.

I sucked my thumb as a child. I always wanted cotton in my hand to rub against my nose. I would call it cottie. Betty would always tell me, "I'll go get you some cottie." But cottie wouldn't comfort me today. I just wanted my mama back. I watched the tears roll down my daddy's face as the quartet sang, The Sweet By and By, and the organist played softly. Our friends and family passed by the casket to get one last look at mama. I never quite understood that. I guess it is closure or something like that. Uncle Ernest walked over to me and picked me up. I knew what he was about to do, and I tried to wiggle out of it. He picked me up so I could see mama. I closed my eyes, because I didn't want to see. If I didn't really see her, then maybe she wasn't really dead. Maybe this was really a bad dream or a nightmare, and I would wake up. It wasn't a dream, but it was a nightmare. I know it is better for us to celebrate rituals in our lives: births, deaths, anniversaries, etc. But it has been difficult to celebrate a birthday without thinking of my mama. Prior to her death, she had written a letter to my dad and her children. With the permission of my dad and my siblings, I will share that letter with you:

Danny, Terry, Bobby and Betty,

I am writing you this letter if God calls me to be with Him. I want to tell you a few things. Mama has suffered a long time and now I am at rest so don't grieve about me. Always love each other and don't ever do any thing wrong.

Always look to God for your help, and boys, if you all have to go to the army, don't let other boys talk you into doing anything wrong. Always say to yourself what Jesus would do, and Betty, when you get married, be a good wife and mother. Find a Christian husband and you will always be happy. Now children, if Daddy decides he wants another wife, be good to her, and she will be good to you. You know he will be lonesome, and he needs someone. If you all have any problems, talk to your Aunt Irma. She will help you do the right thing. Remember I love you very much,

Mother

Daddy was thirty four years old at the time of her death. In the letter, she indicated that she didn't expect daddy to stay alone. He loved her very much and was extremely devoted to her. We understood when he started dating Edith Honeycutt one year later. She was a registered nurse at the hospital. They dated for about a year and a half, and in 1964, they were married. Mrs. Edith was 32 years old when she married Daddy. While they were dating, she would cook supper with us and spend time getting to know us. One evening, they came home, and something was different. They seemed shy, a little timid, so we knew something was up. Dad called us into the living room and said, "Kids, I have some information for you. Edith and I are going to get married. What do you think?" I don't recall any of us thinking, "Dad, how could you do this? How could you do this to mom?"

Dad needed a partner, and we needed a mother. We never called her mom, but she was our mother. Mrs. Edith was the oldest of five children. Her mother had left them at a very early age and she, being the oldest, had to care for the others. She understood responsibility, commitment and hard work. She had worked herself through nursing school at Northwestern and continued caring for her dad even after her brothers married. She had learned through experience, the difficulty in raising four teenagers. At dinner one evening, Mrs. Edith told us that she was not here to replace our mother, but she did want to be our mother.

And she was a good one. But this didn't go without problems. Between the two year period of our mom's death and dad's remarriage, we had learned how to depend on each other even more so than as younger children. It seemed to me to be the toughest on Danny. For two years, he had become the other parent. He had become the second parent, the disciplinarian, the supporter and the defender. But he was angry. I don't think he was angry about being the second parent, but he was angry at mom for dying. He became, what we would call, the black sheep of the family. He was rebellious, hard-headed and angry. Terry, Betty and myself gave Mrs. Edith hardly any trouble. We pretty much accepted her. We didn't have to give her any trouble, Danny gave her enough for all of us. Did I mention that he was also stubborn? Danny was the defender of us. If Mrs. Edith tried to correct us, Danny would try to correct her. That didn't seem to work too well. She was trying to show us that she was the parent, and Danny tried to convince her that he was. I truly believe the phrase, " You're not my mama," was coined by Danny. I sure heard him say it a lot. It wasn't that he didn't like Mrs. Edith, he just thought he could raise us better. Danny's anger seemed to increase and he took it out on anyone who would stand in his way. In the family of dynamics, Danny was the protector. A role he still takes seriously even today.

It is amazing how children can come from the same parents and be so totally different. So was the case with Terry and Danny. Terry was a diplomat, the caretaker and the problem solver. Terry was an honor roll student and active in athletics and associations. Terry had caught on to Dad's philosophy that if you want something in life, then you have to work for it. Terry was the one in the family that always had money. If you ever needed something, you could always go to the bank of Terry. Terry was recruited by Louisiana State University to play football, but he chose to marry his high school sweetheart, Sandra. He always knew what he wanted and went after it. He worked his way through Louisiana College and earned a degree. He became a successful high school football coach. When the government decided we needed no prayer or discipline in the school system, Terry knew it was time to get out, and he did. He carried his strong work ethic into the business world and became a very successful businessman.

My twin sister, Betty, and I spent nine months together in very close quarters, and I had had about all I could stand. I told my mom I needed to be born first. It's been said that twins have a very special bond, stronger than the bond between your other siblings. Although Danny, Terry and I have always been extremely close, Betty and I share a special bond.

Betty and I were five years old, and we were playing in the front yard of our little house. I had a fishing pole with a line and hook attached. I was swinging it around my head in a circle. Around and around. Not attentive that Betty was playing in the yard beside me, the fish hook caught in her right hand. Betty screamed in pain as the fish hook dug deep in her finger. I was terrified as I looked at my sister. Tears running down her face, she looked at me, screaming at the top of her lungs. I put the fishing pole down and ran toward her.

"Betty, please don't die! Please don't die!" It was the first traumatic event in my life. I remember sitting there on the ground as my mom took the fish hook out of her hand. I was only five years old, and remember thinking what was I going to do if my sister dies? I think subconsciously Betty never forgot me hanging her with a fish hook. For the next few years, Betty took advantage of my small size. She had grown and matured a lot quicker than I, and had made the most of the situation. She would always wrestle with me, even though I never wanted to, because I knew I couldn't whip her. She would hold me down while I screamed and kicked. I tried to hit her, but she was so much stronger. She would hold me to the ground until I would surrender. I told her that one day I would be as big as her and that I would get even. And I did.

We were in the eighth grade, and I was outside shooting hoops in our basketball goal. Betty came out and hollered,

"How about a game of one on one? Bet I can beat you."

"You think you can," I said, as I bounced her the ball. I was a little smaller and quicker, and as I would drive past her, headed toward the goal, she would bump me. I had had enough. I chased after her, and I tackled her in the back yard. What a stroke of luck! As she went down, lying on the ground next to her was a pile of cow manure. It had been there for a while, and it was dry. I grabbed a handful and shoved it into her mouth.

"Now take that. You are a sore loser," I said. A real fight was on now. She spit out the dry particles from her mouth. I knew I could outrun and outlast her. I don't know how long we played that cat and mouse game. I knew she was hot. Even though I could whip her, I knew that if she caught me I would take away some bruises and cuts.

Betty is a beautiful woman. She took after our mama. She has black hair, dark eyes and our mother's personality. She's not afraid to defend herself, not afraid to speak her mind, and not afraid to tell me when she thought I was out of line. She used that one quite a lot.

Daddy had four children, and Mrs. Edith had four step-children. But they didn't have any of their own. I have heard that married women talk about an indescribable desire to have a child of their own, to take care of a child for nine months, to nurture. That was an experience Mrs. Edith had never had. But in 1967, we would have the privilege to experience this miracle. Their first child, James Kevin Smith was born.

Kevin was born and raised in a totally different environment than what my four siblings and I had experienced. He had four older sibling to take care of him, to torture him and to play with him. He was like having a new puppy around the house. It didn't take long for us to realize that

Kevin was extremely intelligent. But why wouldn't he be? He had four older siblings to emulate. I remember right after Kevin's birth, friends were over and referred to him as our half brother. They were quickly corrected. Kevin was not our half brother; he was our brother. There was no difference and we treated him as such.

But Kevin was different. Terry, Danny, Betty and I seemed to have picked up on our mother's personality. Quite obviously, Kevin didn't have that blood line. It was hard to determine who he was more like. He was just a little of both Dad and Mrs. Edith. Kevin would grow up to be the largest member of our family at 6'4" and 240 pound range. He is a gentle giant. I would have to consider him, unlike the rest of us, an introvert. Kevin is kind of shy, quiet and handsome. He loves children and the elderly. Where in the world did he get all that patience? From early on, it was obvious that Kevin would probably become a doctor, which he did.

In 1971, we would get the news that Mrs. Edith was once again pregnant. Unfortunately, the second birth would not be as promising as the first. Tests indicated that their un-born little girl, Carla Delynn, was mentally and physically handicapped. She would live only three days after her birth. She would be buried next to our mother. For the next twenty nine years, Daddy and Mrs. Edith would continue to love, honor and support each other. They watched their five children go through marriages, divorce and even death, until Mrs. Edith's death, the day after Mother's Day in 2000. At the writing of this book, my dad is 73, finally retired and enjoying his children, grandchildren and great grandchildren and following the Louisiana College Wildcat girls' basketball team. Go Cats!

CHAPTER 5
SHE WAS MY HIGH SCHOOL
SWEETHEART

It was a somewhat typical day in Louisiana, hot and humid. I was working outside in my shop when I realized it was time to go in and get ready to go to work. I was a Monroe City Police Officer, working the night shift. I stopped and got a glass of water, drank it quickly and continued down the hall into the bedroom. I noticed my wife, Jackie, and our one-year-old daughter, Kim, playing in the living room. I was working the evening shift and roll call started at 3:30 p.m., and I was always early. I jumped in the shower and began to lather up with soap. The door opened and closed, and I heard Jackie as soon as she cleared her throat.

"Bobby, it's 2:30. When you get home in the morning, Kim and I will be gone."

The words ran through my head. Gone. What does she mean she and Kim will be gone? Is she going to her mother's for the weekend to visit? What does she mean she will be gone?

"Bobby, I don't want to live like this. The one thing that is important to you is being a cop. You never have time for me or Kim. It's always about your job or your police buddies."

I stood there with the water continuing to run down my body. The door opened and closed again, and she was gone. Tears began to run down my face. I had no defense. What she was saying was true. This police job had become my number one priority. It had become my lover. I stepped out of the shower, dried off and started putting on my uniform. I always felt so proud when I put that uniform on. That dark blue uniform with the Monroe police department badge. The black leather gear with the Model 19 .357 magnum. Although I was only a first year police officer, I sure felt proud.

I was sitting on the edge of the bed putting on my boots. What does she expect? I worked full time as a police officer, and I went to school full time to earn my degree. When I was off, I was at court or in training. There just didn't seem to be enough time to spend with them. There just didn't seem to be any left over. I finished getting dressed and walked back down the hall where Kim was playing on the floor. I sat down on the floor with her, pulled her into my lap and played with the toy she was playing with. She was going to take Kim away. The thoughts were racing through my head. I gave her a big hug and a kiss.

"Daddy loves you, baby. I will see you later. You be good today." I placed her on the floor and walked to the kitchen where Jackie was standing at the sink.

"Well, Bob, what are you going to do?" she asked.

"I'm going to work because that is what I have to do. I have to go to work."

"That's what I thought you would say," Jackie replied, as I walked out the back door.

The subconscious mind was in full gear as it started dumping the memories of the past into the present. Was I going to become a statistic? Was I going to be one of the 75% of police officers who get divorced? As a rookie police officer, that is what I had always heard. Don't expect to be married very long. You will find that your wife will become this job. Be prepared for that. One for all and all for one. We all stick together. We are the family now. The only friends you will have will be other police officers. You will lose all of your other so-called friends. They won't understand you, but we will. Remember, son, what goes on in this car, stays in this car. What did that mean? Unfortunately, I knew much too well what that meant. Boy, don't talk to your wife. Don't tell her what goes on out here. All it will do is make her afraid. The less you tell her, the better off it will be. Were these all self-fulfilling prophecies? Would we become what we think? I was a twenty-two-year-old police officer with a little more than a year experience. As I turned onto the highway, my mind began to drift.

I was in the sixth grade at Buckeye High School in Louisiana. It was a small country school, and when a student transferred, everyone knew it. Our sixth grade teacher, Mrs. Bridges, spoke up, "Class, I would like to introduce you to our new student, Jackie Crook. Jackie moves to our area from Lake Charles." There were sixty eyes now, peering at Jackie. I am sure that must have been a very embarrassing moment for Jackie. Jackie was tall, thin and extremely cute. She was a straight A student and played in the band. Of course, everyone seemed tall to me. My twin sister, Betty, was at least a good head taller than me.

My brother, Terry, was in junior high, and my older brother, Danny, was a freshman. Both were football players and both were extremely talented. Naturally, I was expected to play as well. But did I mention that I was really small? Several weeks would pass, and then an announcement came out. Anyone interested in playing in the band, please report to the band room in fifth hour. A light came on in my head. I would really get to know her then. She plays in the band, and I think I will play in the band too. Or so I thought. The band director, Mr. Martinez, let the students try different band instruments. He figured I would be good at the baritone. It just had three buttons. Surely I could figure out how to make a sound out of three buttons. I wasn't very good at band, and as a matter of fact, I only lasted a couple of weeks. Of course, Terry and Danny made sure that I never learned to read a note in band. I was sitting outside at my house one afternoon after school. Terry and Danny came in after football practice. There I was, sitting with my baritone in my lap, trying to learn how to read those notes. I was trying. My two brothers stepped out of the car and walked over to me. "What are you doing there, Toot-toot?"

"I'm trying to learn how to read these notes so I can play in the band." Danny took the instrument out of my hand and began to take it apart.

"What are you doing?"

"Bobby, you ain't playing in the band. We're football players and so are you."

"But Danny, I'm too little to play football. There's no way I can play it."

"You'll play football." He continued taking apart my instrument, put it back in its case and then he shut it. He handed it back to me. "Now there is your baritone instrument. Now take it back to school and trade it in for football cleats."

So much for my band career. The next day, I did as I was told. Luckily for me, Jackie's family moved into our neighborhood. She went to the same church I went to. Jackie and I became friends. My girlfriend. One afternoon after school, we had a pep rally. Jackie was playing in the pep rally. I walked her back from the pep rally to the band room to put up her instrument, we then had to catch the bus. We were standing outside the band room, and I worked up enough courage to reach over and kiss her. It was my first kiss.

I was not a very good student, a C average at best,

at my very best. This year would not be a good one though, because on December 12, my mother would die on my tenth birthday. I was socially promoted to the sixth grade, although I didn't successfully complete that class. I would fail and have to repeat it then I would fail again, and they would socially promote me again. We didn't have counseling back then; not for students and not for anyone else, as I recall. When you lost someone, you just move along with life. I was only ten years old. How do you move along with life when you lose your mama? My junior high years would not be much better. I would struggle academically. I would fail the seventh grade, and I would go to summer school to make up for the courses that I had failed.

The high school years would be a little better. Jackie and I continued to date. We dated our way through high school. I did play sports a little bit. I got a little bit bigger but not much, and I was an average athlete at best. Jackie was a majorette. We were elected class favorites several times during junior high and high school.

In August of 1971, Jackie and I got married. Jackie went on to nursing school while I went to work a trade. I had worked in building construction during the summers, and I went to work as a construction helper. I would later go to work as an electrician, while Jackie finished up school at Louisiana State University at Alexandria in nursing. I decided that I would give college a shot. My fifth grade teacher, Mrs. Bridges, talked to a friend, Wallace McCann, who I was going to LSUA with at the time. He had told her about some of the students from Buckeye going to college, and he had mentioned my name.

Mrs. Bridges said, "He's going to college. You must be joking. There is no way he could make it through college. Wallace, you should tell him that he just needs to learn a trade. He's not college material."

Mrs. Bridges will never know how those words rang in my ears. I completed one year of university at LSUA then transferred to Northeast Louisiana University in Monroe, Louisiana. Jackie would go to work as an emergency room nurse, and the following year, I would go to work at the Monroe Police Department. Our work and my school began to weigh heavily on our marriage.

I hadn't spent enough time with Jackie and Kim, and today that was coming to a head. Within a few days, Jackie had moved out and into her own apartment. Jackie and I would stay separated over the next year. We talked about getting back together from time to time. But I had developed that police mentality; all for one and one for all. I was just another statistic. I might as well go ahead and get it out of the way. One of the police personality characteristics is that we usually marry our high school sweethearts the first time around.

CHAPTER 6
HOW ABOUT THOSE COPING SKILLS?

I have been told that police officers usually are divorced. But I never heard anyone mention how tough it would be. I missed Jackie and Kim tremendously. I missed coming in from work, eating dinner, and playing with Kim. That would take its toll. I started coping with my losses the best I could. In the last two years, I had quite obviously met a lot of police officers, and they had taught me how to drink.

Joseph Wambaugh has written a book called Choir Boys. It was a policeman's bible on how to cope with stress on the job. It was very simple: after you get off work everyday, you need to unwind. Go get a couple of beers with the boys, and that will take care of all the stress. You could drink away all the murders, rapes and police officers getting killed across the country. If you don't want to deal with all the losses, then get another drink. We will dull the pain and numb the losses. That way, it didn't really happen. The subconscious mind is pretty powerful. It takes in all that happens in our lives, seven day a week, twenty-four hours a day. It just logs all those memories in the subconscious mind. The ones that are too hard to deal with, it just shuts them away in a closet, a real small closet. We shut the door on it and lock it. We try to keep it locked, so we don't have to deal with the pain, death, sadness and grief.

I remember watching a Fram oil filter commercial. The mechanic was standing there holding an orange Fram oil filter in his hand. To his left, was an automobile with the hood raised up with smoke billowing out. As he held the oil filter in his hand, he began to talk about the importance of changing the filter in the engine on a regular basis. If you will just change this filter out on a regular basis, keep the oil clean in the engine, and keep the dirty oil dumped out, then your engine will run more effectively and run longer. But you have a choice. You can pay me now, as he pointed to the oil filter, or you can pay me later, as he pointed to the car with the engine that was burnt up. As a result of our police mentality, as we are usually in control, police officers usually pay for it later, and it is a lot more costly. Cops don't like to talk about their fears and the losses that they endure every day, we just block it out. It's not cool for cops to talk about our problems. It's a sign of weakness. I, along with a couple of my friends, would start hitting the partying circuit. Partying and girls. Anything to fill the void. We would do anything to keep our mind from thinking about our losses. Drinking, girls, riding motorcycles, rodeoing, parachuting, anything we could possibly do to keep our minds off our problems. We loved living on the edge.

I was a country boy. I grew up riding horses. Growing up in the country, there were always horses, and we were constantly breaking someone's horses. I thought, why not break a few bulls. I had met Sammy Pace, who was majoring in agricultural business. He was a bull rider. I liked the way Sammy looked with his blue jeans, can of Skoal in his back pocket and ten gallon hat. I had met Sammy in one of my classes in college, and he asked me if I wanted to go to a rodeo with him one night. Sure, why not, it has been a long time since I have been to a rodeo. To me, the most important part of a rodeo was the bull rider. Boy, what courage they must have to climb on the back of a 2,000 pound bull, strap a rope around its front girth, take another rope and throw it around the back girth and cinch up his gonads real tight. Some fool would swing open the gate. Another cow-boy would shock him with a Hot Shock and off he would go with that cowboy hanging on. He just had to hang on for eight seconds. Eight seconds. That didn't seem like such a hard thing. I was about as good at bull riding as I was with sports: average at best. But it sure was fun, and man, was it exciting! Also, did I mention it was very dangerous?

I would rodeo for a couple of years. I traveled to dif-ferent small rodeos with my friends. Sometimes I would take Kim along, and she would sit on the rail and watch as dad-dy rode the bulls, or at least, tried to ride them. The PRCA rodeo was in town in Monroe, and my roommate, Dennis Cook, had gone to that rodeo on Friday night. I was signed up for that rodeo too. It would be my last. Dennis came in from the rodeo that Friday night, and I was sitting in the den, watching television.

"Man, Bobby, you should have been here tonight. It was wild. There was this one bull named Mighty Mouse. It was bucking and jumping, and it jumped over one chute into another chute with a rider on top of the bull. They had to open up the gates to let the bulls out, and Mighty Mouse started running around the arena, hooking bulls, chasing the clowns and hooking the cowboys on horseback. He went berserk. They finally got him in the back holding pen with the other bulls, but he was going crazy. It was a riot! You should have been there. It was a beautiful thing."

"Wow, sounds exciting. I hate I missed that."

"What bull are you riding tomorrow?"

"I don't know. I will find out when I get there."

I would arrive at the rodeo arena early that eve-ning and check the charts to see what bull I was riding. I ran my finger down the list to see what bull I had drawn. Bobby Smith, hometown cowboy, had drawn: you guessed it! Mighty Mouse! I swallowed hard when I read that name. You've got to be joking. The first event was bull riding. They began to load the bulls in the six chutes. I slid over onto the back of Mr. Mighty Mouse himself. I slipped my hand in the ropes, and the adrenaline began to rush through my body. At least, that is what we call it, but it's really fear. But that is the part I liked as a cop, living on the edge. Mighty Mouse turned around and looked straight at me. His eyes were blood red. I looked up and said, "Man, did you see that, this sucker is the devil himself!"

It was a Jim Shoulders' PRCA rodeo. Jim Shoulders, himself, was pulling my gate. He began to holler, "Let's go! Let's go! Let's go! C'mon, we are running late. Let's go, cowboy. Are you gonna sit up there all day like it's a rocking chair?"

I nodded my head. Mighty Mouse jumped out like a wild freight train, bucking and diving everywhere. I was holding on like a monkey on a dog. Cameras were flashing. The crowd was cheering, but it wasn't long before I hit the ground. My first thought was "where was the darn bull?" I wanted to make sure he wasn't going to run up my back. Then I heard the horn sound, which was not a good sound. That means you didn't make it. I picked up my hat and rope and started back toward the chute. The clown came over and said, "Better luck next time, cowboy."

There will not be a next time. I have had just about all the nonsense I could stand. See you later, buddy.

I wasn't like all the other police officers. I wasn't into the guns, shooting and riding motorcycles. I wasn't like that, but I did need more excitement in my life. I'd given up bull riding, but I needed something equally as challenging and dangerous. Something where I could put my life on the line and still call it fun. I had asked to be transferred to narcotics at Monroe Police Department. I didn't get chosen, and I was pretty aggravated and kind of let down. I was told that I would get transferred along with my friend, Pat Stewart. Pat had been transferred to narcotics, and I wanted to go with him. But it didn't happen. I guess sometimes police officers can act like spoiled little kids. I had my feelings hurt that I didn't get chosen. As a matter of fact, I felt that the person who was chosen wasn't a better choice than me. The West Monroe Police Department was looking for a narcotic agent, and in a last ditch effort, I went to talk to our chief to see if I could go to narcotics. He said the choice had been made. Did I mention that police officers are usually impatient? I went to talk to West Monroe police chief, Larry LaBorde, and I told him I was interested in becoming a narcotic agent. He told me to take the test, and he would love to have me. I did, and was hired in the narcotics division. Man, that was a different world, and it was fun. I let my hair grow out, grew me a beard, and I started learning the narcotic lingo. Buying dope and hanging out with dealers. Sitting in bars in the wee hours of the morning, trying to buy dope.

Chief LaBorde called me and gave me my first real assignment: sitting on a load of dope so a violator would come pick it up. Chief said he wanted to do some surveillance and then make the arrest. Surveillance. I had heard about that at the academy, but never done it. Man, you have to have the patience of the pope to do surveillance. Sit on a load of dope for hours and sometimes days at a time. That was pretty much what happened. They dropped me off in a wooded area where the dope had been dropped off. There I was, all by myself, nothing but a walkie-talkie in my hand. I was sitting a safe distance from the dope, waiting for a violator to come get it, so they could make the delivery. Man, how big the mosquitoes are around here! You had to be still and inconspicuous, waiting for the car of dope dealers to arrive. I looked at my watch. 5:15 p.m. Man, how many days have I been here? Oh, only fifteen minutes! Well, it seemed like days. Seven more hours would pass. I felt like a cat tied upside down, hanging from a tree limb. I was about to lose my sanity. I picked up my walkie-talkie and called Sergeant Pat Kelly.

"Pat, are you there?"

"I'm here, Bob. Go ahead."

I said, "Do ya'll see any action anywhere?"

"No, nothing is going on. It's still pretty quiet. Nobody's come yet, huh, Bobby?"

"Nope, just me, the squirrels and the armadillos. How much longer are we gonna have to sit on this thing before we call it off?"

Pat laughed into the walkie-talkie. "Welcome to narcotics."

Well, so much for relieving my stress. The hours were long with long days in court, lots of paperwork and filling out warrants. The work never seemed to end. I found myself working day and night. But I was sure having fun. It's not enough that we as police officers use alcohol to numb our stresses, but now I was working for a department where you were being paid to drink. I was hanging out in bars with the scum of the earth. I found myself drinking a lot more, even when I was off. It was always better before you went to bed; it would help you sleep better. It would help numb the pain.

"Headquarters, P 11."

"P 11, go ahead."

"Bobby, 10-19 to the station. They need you to come by and see the sergeant. They have a call that they want you to go on."

I was only a few moments from the station. I pulled in and met Sgt. Kelly.

"Bobby, we've got a man with a knife. He's strung out on LSD, and the mother is calling us. He's standing outside a second story window and threatening everyone who comes into the room."

I thought, that's great. That's what I want to do, go fight a crazy who is strung out on drugs. I walked to my desk and picked up the phone to call Pat Stewart.

"Pat, meet me at this location. We have a man with a knife who is strung out on LSD, and they want us to go talk to him before he kills himself or someone else."

Pat and I arrived at the scene. There were marked units there who escorted us to the apartment. The mother was hysterical, standing in the doorway, saying, "Ya'll please help my son. He just needs some help."

Yeah, I'd say he does. The man was squatted in the window, cursing and screaming threats. Pat and I walked in wearing no uniform. We were just a couple of guys with long hair.

Maybe he thought to himself, "Well, they kinda look like me. Maybe they are our friends."

I guess I was destined to go into the mental health field and counseling/psychology, because every time there was a scene, they always called me to go talk to them. Or maybe they just considered I was as crazy as the rest of them. I began to talk to the man to get him to step out of the window. I tried to make him see how very important life was, and that he was probably just going through a really hard time. But we were there to help.

"We're going to get you some help. You've just had a string of bad luck. Man, we have all had those times. Man, I am just here to help you. Why don't you just step out of that window?"

You could almost see his face begin to distort and change right there before us. His eyes looked like they were glazing over. He stepped down out of the window, stuck his knife out and said, "Now I am fixing to kill you S.O.B.'s."

Yeah, buddy. That's where I want to be. I want to be in an apartment building, with a crazed LSD user, with a knife in his hand, trying to take our lives. You better do some fast talking now, brother.

The man started walking towards us. We began to talk, screaming for some reinforcement from the officer standing in the door. I sure hoped someone remembered how to take a knife away from somebody, because I dang sure didn't. The fight was on. Someone had struck the man with a night stick across his hand, and the weapon went to the floor. We took him down, and it took five of us to get him handcuffed. He was stronger than an ox. They finally took him out, and Pat and I walked to the car and started driving off. My hands were still trembling. I was scared to death. Pat was a Vietnam veteran and had been in situations worse than this many times. He seemed to be pretty calm.

"Pat, how in the world do you deal with something like that? Man, do you realize that we could have been killed?"

"Yep, I guess it's all part of the job whether we like it or not."

To protect and to serve, even if it means us losing our lives. As we drove back to the office, the reality began to sink in.

I turned to Pat once again. "Pat, have you ever thought about it? What would happen if you got shot or killed in the line of duty?"

"Nope, I guess I don't think about it, Bobby. That's

something I guess I don't want to think about."

"But Pat, we could have been killed this weekend. Did you think about that?"

"Yeah, buddy, that's just not something we talk about. Sometimes you just gotta suck it up and get it."

Suck it up and get it. Yeah, that's what they say. Let's just put another stressor in the closest and slam that door shut and have a few more drinks, and yeah, it will all go away. Won't it? No sir, it doesn't go away. As a matter of fact, research shows us that nearly three times the number of police officers killed in the line of duty would take their own life. On average, 350 or 400 police officers would commit suicide. Why? It's pretty simple. No one ever told us it was okay to talk about our problems. No one ever told us it was okay to dump the water out of the glass every evening before going home without using a glass of whiskey. No one ever told us it was okay to sit down with our clergy or a best friend or a counselor, for heaven's sake and heaven forbid, talking to our spouse. So we keep on with the dysfunctional behavior: drinking, overeating, undereating, sleep disturbances and feeling like we have to sleep all the time to deal with the depression or not being able to sleep at all. Too many of us develop insomnia. We want to sleep all the time, or we don't sleep at all. We don't eat, or we eat all the time. We are looking for something to soothe us, something to satisfy us. Still looking for something to soothe, or gratify, we look for it in sex or then, the extreme opposite of this, impotence. I have yet to find a police officer who will admit to that. We are too macho to admit that we aren't ready at any given moment. But that is what we were taught. If you were stressed, get you a drink, a woman or a little bit more sleep, and it will all work out. But it doesn't work out, and I keep remembering the Fram oil filter. Why don't they tell us about the right coping mechanism? Or the importance of exercise? Working out three or four times a week for an hour or so. Just to dump some of the water out of the glass in an appropriate setting. Or how about relaxation? Police officers relax? You've got to be joking. Too many closets full of pain, and fear, and agony, and death. We've got to keep those doors closed. It's too painful to open those doors. I am convinced that after twenty five years in law enforcement, we cannot make it in this job by ourselves. We have to look to one another to ask for help. Remember, we are only human.

CHAPTER 7
DEBBIE WOULD BE NUMBER TWO

It was October, and the county fair was coming to town. We always loved the county fair. Popcorn, cotton candy, chili dogs and elephant ears. It was fun watching the different types of people who come in. You have those that actually work, who brought in the livestock to show. It was all business to them. Then you have the spectators who just gawk around a bit. They don't know the difference between a bull, a cow, a goat or a sheep. It was incredible to see their ignorance. But it was always fun to watch the children. They would run through the fair with cotton candy on their faces and get on the rides with sticky fingers. You could see the excitement on their faces. But that's not the ones we got to deal with. We got to deal with the troublemakers. The ones who were there to steal, get drunk and disrupt everyone's fun. We had been assigned to the night shift. We had made the rounds, talked to people and ate a couple of hot dogs. You know, the things police officers are supposed to do.

I was walking through the arena where all the displays are located, and spotted a friend of mine: Trooper Danny Warner. He was standing in front of a photography studio, talking to the owner. As I was talking to Danny, I spotted a picture of a young lady. A huge picture. Miss Louisiana Teenager. Wow! What a knockout! Dark hair, brown eyes, olive complexion, and a big beautiful smile. Man, she looked good.

"Who's that?" I said.

Danny turned around. "Who's who?"

"The girl in the picture. Miss Louisiana Teenager."

"Her name is Debbie. You want to meet her?"

"Sure, why not."

"Well, she's not here tonight, but she will probably be here one night. How long are you working?"

"I'll be here all week."

"Well, if she comes by, I will holler at you. Ya'll would make a cute couple."

"Yeah, yeah, yeah." I stood around talking to other people as they walked by.

Several other people commented, "Who's the girl in the picture? Gosh, she sure is pretty."

It seemed to be the talk around the photography studio on how pretty this girl was.

The fair had come and gone, and we were back in our routine. I was sitting in my house one evening when the phone rang.

"Hello."

"Hey, Bobby, this is Danny. Remember the picture of the girl you saw at the fair?"

"Yeah, I remember. A good looking girl."

"Well, I ran into her a few days ago. I told her all about you, how good looking you are and everything." He chuckled on the other end.

"Oh, you think that's funny, huh?"

"Well, I lied about you and told her what a great guy you were and everything. She said that she would like to meet you. She wants you to give her a call. Do you have something to write with?"

"Sure, give me a second." I grabbed a pen and a piece of paper and wrote down her number. She worked at the photography studio, and I gave her a call. The phone rang. A cheerful voice answered, "Hello, photography studio. This is

Debbie. May I help you?"

"I sure hope so. This is Bobby Smith. A mutual friend of ours, Danny Warner, told me he talked to you and to give you a call."

"Sure, Bobby, I am kind of busy right now, but maybe call back later."

"Well, how about lunch one day?"

"Give me a call."

She told me when she would be back at work. I waited a few days and then I called her back. "Hey, Debbie, this is Bobby. Whatcha got planned for lunch tomorrow?"

She told me that she was free. I told her that I would pick her up, and we would have lunch.

Debbie was even prettier in person than in the picture. She was very delightful and outgoing. She laughed a lot. She loved to joke and have fun. Her personality was much like mine. I wanted this relationship to work out. We started dating. It seemed like it was going to be a good thing. We both enjoyed sports and going to football games. We played tag football on Sunday afternoon. Debbie was on a softball team, and I was on a softball team as well. We enjoyed the same things. Debbie was a social bug. She enjoyed the social activities. She enjoyed the parties, the drinking, and was in a sorority at the university.

Our relationship was fun and exciting. We were always on the go: partying, going to the beach and having fun. We laughed a lot, and it was fun. But all that glitters is not gold. Although we were getting serious about our relationship, it all seemed to be so surface. It was about looking good and displaying ourselves well in public. There were problems too. Debbie was what we would call a head turner. When she walked into a room, she was so attractive, it would make any male in the room look at her. This would cause some problems. Although when we were together, we seemed to have lots of fun, there was a restlessness in Debbie. She always seemed to be looking for something better. Always looking for greener grass in other pastures. I guess no one ever told her that every pasture needs mowing.

Debbie came from a divorced family. Her dad was a career military man and lived in a different state. He rarely ever spent time with Debbie during childhood. I had met her dad; he was very professional. He had remarried and had three boys, all teenagers by this time. It seemed to be the Cleaver family. I liked her dad. He was a pretty sharp guy. Now her mom, that is a story. What a piece of work! Debbie's mom had divorced her dad when Debbie was extremely young. Her stepdad was killed in an airplane crash. Her mom was on husband number three. Both she and he handled their stressors in life through a bottle. They must have had a lot of stressors. It seemed to me that Debbie could never do anything good enough to please her mom. She was always trying harder.

Debbie had dropped out of school her sophomore year at the university. She started working full time at the bank and was going up the ladder. She was doing well at the bank and gaining experience in the banking industry. But Debbie was always looking for another pasture. Don't get me wrong, I'm no saint either. I had already been through one failed marriage. I didn't want to go through another. I've had my flings as well. A registered nurse. A flight attendant. A physical education major at the university.

Her name was Fran. Prior to meeting Fran, I had given Debbie an engagement ring. Several months later, she returned it to me. She had found another pasture. I was working narcotics, and a friend of mine was going to school at the university. She had asked me to come talk to a physical education association there on the availability and use of drugs in the athletic world. The classroom was packed with athletes. They were all there. In the back of the room was a tall, thin and blonde-haired young lady. As I continued to lecture, I found myself continuing to make eye contact with the blonde in the back.

I would later find out her name was Fran. Several days passed, one of my fellow officers, Bobby Brasher, saw me in the hall and said that I had made quite an impression on one of the students in the lecture.

"Oh, I did, did I? Well, who was it?"

"Her name is Fran."

"So who is Fran?"

He began to describe her to me, and I thought, surely this cannot be the same girl. Not the one I was thinking about, but it was. One thing about being in police circles is that everyone seems to know someone that the other one knows.

"I got her number," Bobby said. "If you want to give her a call. I have known her for a long time. I think ya'll will enjoy each other."

I gave Fran a call and asked if she wanted to go out on the weekend. She told me she was graduating on December 12.

"Wow, that is my birthday," I told her.

"I'm having dinner with my mom, sister and dad after graduation. But after that, I will meet you somewhere."

We decided on the location. A couple of my friends and their dates met us. She was delightful. She was kind of shy and quiet, especially for a P.E. major. It was the beginning of a one-year relationship. I was learning things about myself. I needed someone. I needed someone permanently. I didn't like going out with a bunch of girls. The dating game, it just wasn't my game. Fran and I both had lots of things in common as well. She liked to play basketball, and I enjoyed that as well. I worked out, and she would come with me. On weekends, we would go out with our friends or go up to her parent's house. They lived about twenty five miles from town, in the country. Her mom and dad were my kind of people. Her sister, Jill, was three years younger than Fran. It didn't take me long to become part of their family. Fran and Jill were their only two children, and her dad had always wanted a son. There were rumors around town that I would be his new son-in-law. Her dad was a gentleman. He was very quiet, kind, and compassionate. We quickly became friends.

It was in the fall. I helped her dad cut down trees and fix a fence. It was just like being at home as a child. We were outside one afternoon, stacking firewood against the house. He threw me the keys to his truck and said, "Let me show you something." We drove down the road and turned off down a dirt road. We had to slow down, and he told me to turn off a little dirt road. We drove for awhile and pulled up to a metal gate. We stopped and got out.

"What are we doing?"

"Hand me that welder out of the truck," he said. There was a problem with the gate that needed to be fixed. He grabbed his keys and unlocked the lock.

"I want to show you something," he said. There was no road leading in. Just land, just beautiful land. Big trees and bushes everywhere as we weaved our way through.

"Where are we going?" I asked.

"I want to show you something. Go a little further and then stop." As we drove up to a clearing, there was a small pond sitting there.

"Man, this would be a great place for a house," he said.

"It sure would be. This is beautiful."

He turned to me and said, "Bob, if you and Fran get married, this piece of land is yours. I am going to give it to you."

"Wow, is this too good to be true?" Are you tempting me or bribing me or what?

I didn't understand then about attachments in relationships, and how sometimes, even years later, you can feel that attachment. You get emotionally attached. I felt extremely committed to Fran, yet I would find myself thinking about Debbie. I wondered how she was doing. She would think the same thing. She would call me and see how I was doing. I thought it was quite harmless, but the effect was extremely devastating to my relationship with Fran. It stirred up a lot of emotional garbage. It was extremely confusing. Debbie didn't want me, but she didn't want anyone else to have me either. Debbie and I were both in other relationships, but we still kept talking. It kept us from making a serious commitment to anyone. I truly loved Fran, but my love/hate relationship I had with Debbie was extremely destructive and very confusing. I had to step back from our relationship and see what was going on. Living in a small town it didn't take long for it to get back to Fran that Debbie and I were talking. She gave me an ultimatum.

"It's either me or her," she said. "Bobby, I love you, but I won't settle for you part time."

At least, she had the courage to say that. There were lots of changes taking place in my life that didn't help. I was preparing for graduation. I was about to be a college graduate. How about that, Mrs. Bridges? I had been a cop for six years, which is a point where cops decide if this is a career for them. To see if this is good for them or if they need to try something else. I left the police department and applied for a job in Lafayette with Baroid Industries. It was a chemical company that supplied chemicals for oil and gas production industry. There was a job opening up in Houma, Louisiana. I thought this would be a good chance to get away from police work, my relationship with Debbie and Fran, and go somewhere and clear my head. I found out that you can't run from your problems. I interviewed for the job and got it. I moved to Houma, and it was a six or seven hour drive from Monroe where I lived at the time and where my daughter also lived. This would be a serious problem for me.

Debbie and I started seeing each other again. We were even talking about marriage. I couldn't get Fran off my mind. Although Debbie's mom didn't think very highly of me, my family loved Debbie. I felt pressure to work out my issues with Debbie from my family, Debbie and some of my friends. Since I was moving to south Louisiana, why didn't I go ahead and get married and try to get my life straight? It all sounded good to me. I wished it would be that simple. But there again, this macho police officer didn't have the courage to say no to the job or relationship. I took the job and moved down to Houma. Our district office was in Lafayette, home of University of Southwestern Louisiana. The same university where Fran had been accepted to graduate school. I hadn't talked to Fran in several months, and Debbie and I had talked about setting a date for our wedding. I knew deep in my heart that this wedding was a mistake. Why couldn't I just say no? What was it about Debbie that had such an emotional hold on me that I couldn't let go?

I was sitting in my office one afternoon. I couldn't get Fran off my mind. Debbie and I had set a date for October. It was the latter part of September. I picked up the phone and called her. "Fran, this is Bobby. I really need to talk to you. Could I meet you in Lafayette and eat lunch?" Reluctantly, she said yes.

We set a time and date. I drove over on a Sunday afternoon and we had lunch. It didn't take long for the conversation to get serious.

"I understand that you and Debbie are getting married."

"That's what I want to talk to you about. I really need to know how you feel. I need to tell you how I feel about you."

I felt like such a Judas with both Fran and Debbie. I was just trying to find a way out. I needed some help in making the right decision.

"Fran, marrying Debbie is a mistake, and I know that. I don't know how to say no. I don't know how to make the ball stop rolling. I need to know how you feel. It's not fair to make everyone go through with this wedding, but I need to know how you feel."

Fran began to cry. That surely didn't help. It broke my heart. I reached out to touch her hand to comfort her, but she pulled away.

"You've made your choice, now you can live with it." She got up and stormed from the table.

Three weeks would pass. Dealing with an LSD junkie in the window was easier than this. Pat Stewart and I, dressed in white tuxes, were standing in front of the church. The music was playing. The wedding was on. I was only six feet away from the door.

I turned to Pat. "This is a mistake. I can't go through with this. I'm in love with Fran. It's not fair to me or her or Debbie. I can't go through with this."

Pat began to freak out. "Bobby, you can't do this. It's too late."

"It's not too late. Better to walk out now than later.

I am just going to leave. Tell the pastor that I changed my mind." I stormed to the door. My car was only twenty steps away when Pat grabbed me by the arm and pulled me back.

"Bobby, you can't do this. You can't do this to everyone else. To your family. To her family. It just ain't right."

The pastor walked out of his office then and asked if we were ready. I heard the march beginning. It was a march alright. It was a march of doom. We walked out and stood in front of the church. Me, Pat, and the pastor. Kim came walking down the aisle. She was a flower girl. She was so cute, walking down the aisle and throwing her petals out with her big smile.

I stood there telling myself that it was going to be okay. I was just a little screwed up in the head. It was all going to work out. Debbie walked down the aisle and stood next to me. As the pastor conducted the ceremony, he told us to repeat the wedding vows. To have and hold. In sickness and in health. To love and to cherish. Until death do you part. Man, those are some powerful words. Unfortunately, we don't take them seriously. But I was going to try to take them seriously. We both said I do.

I was in chemical school in Texas. I had gotten married on the weekend, and I had to be back in class on Monday. After the wedding reception, Debbie and I would drive to Houston, Texas. It was a long drive, and I had a long time to think. It was late at night, and Debbie had fallen asleep. Everything was silent. Too much time to think. What in the world have I done? I looked over at her, watching her sleep. It was so unfair what I had done to her. We arrived at the hotel late that night. We unpacked our bags and went into the hotel. Debbie had taken a shower and gotten in bed.

"Are you coming to bed?" she said.

"No," I said, pulling out my briefcase. "I've got some

homework that I need to get done. I'm not even prepared for class. I need to get this done for class." I just needed a distraction. I needed to escape. I didn't want to face the reality of what I had done. I had married a woman that I wasn't in love with. I didn't know what to do.

Debbie sat up in bed. "Bobby, something's wrong. Tell me what is wrong."

I faced Debbie, making eye contact. I said, "Debbie, I am so sorry. I have made a mistake. We shouldn't have gotten married."

Yes, I was a jerk for not having the courage to say no when I needed to have said no. But I had said yes tonight. I had said yes to a commitment, and I wondered how in the world I would keep that commitment.

Debbie started crying. "What do you want me to do?"

"I don't know. I just feel like we made a mistake."

"I'll go back home tomorrow and get the marriage annulled. If this is how you feel, I surely don't want to be married to you."

"I don't blame you, and I understand."

I was getting ready to go back to school. I said that I would drive her to the airport and get her a ticket to go home.

"Bobby, I think we should at least give it a try."

I had one more week of school left, and then we drove back home to our new home in Houma. I returned back to the office to find a letter sitting on my desk. It was from Fran.

"By now," she wrote, "you and Debbie are probably married, and I wish you the best. I just want you to know that I will always love you and I still do."

So many emotions raced through me. I was angry, a part of me was a little happy. It was too little, too late. I was married. What am I supposed to do now? Why, Fran? Why did you have to do this?

I don't think you have to be a rocket scientist to figure out where this marriage is going to go. For the next year, Debbie and I struggled in our relationship to try to make things work out. But there were other problems on top of that. I missed Kim tremendously. The drive was hard, and I found myself seeing her just periodically. It wasn't near enough. She needed her daddy and I needed my little girl. I wanted to transfer to north Louisiana, which caused another problem because Debbie was extremely jealous of Kim. She didn't like the time Kim and I spent together. When we did spend time together, she made it as hard for all of us as she possibly could. I went by the state police office to pick up an application. At least I was happy working there, and it was the best paying job I ever had. I just wanted to be a cop again. I moved back to Monroe and became a construction worker for a year. Our marriage continued to be a roller coaster ride, ups and downs, ups and downs. At least being a state trooper again would help out. I could spend more time with Kim and see her more often. I'd get off from work at 3:30 p.m. I would slip on gym shorts and tennis shoes. I went running every afternoon. I was lifting weights and working out, so I could be in top shape for the academy.

I had taken my state police exam and made a 93 out of a 100. That was a pretty good score, and I felt good about it. Jackie Coleman, who worked for the West Monroe police department while I was in Monroe, was also accepted. Jackie and I went from Baton Rouge to Monroe many times together. The exams, the interviews, and let us not forget about the physical fitness agility tests. Although I was a competitive powerlifter at the time, I had been an athlete all my life. I had one serious problem. I had had four operations on my right knee as a result of playing sports. Jackie and I were talking about the physical fitness exam coming up. I talked to him about my concern on whether or not they would pass me.

"Bobby Smith, step in here."

It was a rough voice. A voice of authority. Aubrey Futrell. When I walked into the room, what an intimidator he was.

"Have a seat on the table, son."

They began to poke and prod. The state police department physician measured me, took my blood pressure and checked my heart rate. Then Aubrey saw the eight inch scar that ran across my right knee. I told him that I had all the cartilage removed in the four surgeries. He looked at me with a frown on his face. "No, there is no way you will make it, son. There's no way this knee can stand the fitness regimen at the state police."

I said, "Mr. Futrell, I am a competitive power lifter. I am an athlete. I run all the time, I work out all the time. I know my knee can take it."

"That's nothing to what you would go through here. I'm sorry, but we are rejecting you."

We drove back to Monroe. Jackie and I didn't talk a whole lot. I immediately got in and typed another application. Within a couple of hours, I mailed it. I was applying again to the state police, and I hadn't even received my rejection letter yet. I was determined to be a Louisiana State Trooper. Within a couple of weeks, I received a date to start the second process of becoming a state trooper. It was the same process. The written exams, the interviews, and then I showed up in the office in Baton Rouge and looked at Aubrey again.

"Bobby, what are you doing back here?"

"I want to talk to you about something, and don't say

anything until I am finished." I sat up on the table while Aubrey looked at my knee.

"Now what has changed since last time?"

"Nothing, sir. But I know that I will make it through if you just give me a chance."

Aubrey just stood there, saying nothing. He just stared at me, bewildered. He walked over to a cabinet and pulled out a form. "Read this and sign it," he said.

The form said that if I got injured while participating in the physical fitness part then I would have to resign. I signed my name. I jumped off the table with a smile on my face.

"Mr. Futrell, you will not be disappointed."

The trip back to Monroe from Baton Rouge with Jackie was totally different than the one we took before.

Jackie came up and blew his horn. I loaded my suitcase into the back of his car. We started the first of many trips to Baton Rouge as Louisiana state troopers. There was about sixty of us milling around the parking lot that afternoon. No one really knew what was going to happen. Then across the parking lot, five state police cars pulled up. State troopers got out with their training caps on and began to scream and yell. "Fall out, fall out, fall out!" We were like a bunch of chickens running around. Just total chaos.

"I said to fall out!"

It reminded me of Gomer Pyle, USMC. I felt like Gomer Pyle in that moment because I was thinking, "well, golly, what have I gotten myself into?" We finally got into formation.

"You will refer to me as sir, do you understand?"

"Yes, sir."

Not a single one of us was in unison, and that was not cool. I had been called names I was never called before.

I was being given instructions on how and when to do things properly. We were now owned by the Louisiana State Police. You could feel the excitement. Man, this is exciting!

We started each morning early at 5:30 a.m. with calisthenics and physical training with Aubrey Futrell, no less. Aubrey could bench press a Mack truck and run without stopping and he expected us to follow his lead. Weeks would pass, and we would begin to learn how to become Louisiana State Troopers. The program was demanding. Some would not make it. Some don't need to. I was chosen president of my cadet class by my peers. Seventeen weeks later, we had completed our course. It was graduation day. I stood at the podium as president of my class, addressing my peers. Not since the birth of Kim had I felt such excitement, exhilaration and pride. I was a Louisiana State Trooper.

We were assigned and supposed to report to our troops. I was assigned to Troop F in Monroe. At 7:30 a.m. on Monday morning, Jackie Coleman and I, along with other state troopers, stood in the lobby waiting for the captain to call us in to give us our assignments. What counties would we be assigned to? As luck would have it, Jackie and I were assigned to the same county. Tensas County was a rural county with three small cities, Newellton, St. Joseph and Waterproof. The county was spread out for miles and miles over farm land. It was cotton and bean fields. Jackie and I found our way to the sheriff's office. Sheriff Poe was the sheriff there and his son, Billy, was a captain with the Louisiana State Police and assigned to headquarters. Jackie and I introduced ourselves, and he took us around introducing us to his staff.

"This will be your office right here," he said, pointing to a small office in a trailer space. "If you need anything, let me know. Good luck, boys. Don't be too hard on my people out there."

It didn't take too long in a small town for everyone to get to know who we were. Jackie was a good cop. He was laid back and methodical. He didn't miss anything. Me, on the other hand. I was just having fun being a state trooper. We wouldn't have made it through those days without Roger and Bonnie Jaubert. Roger was a deputy at the sheriff's department. We didn't know anyone there and they invited us over many times for lunch and dinner. I was making friends in Tensas Parish, trying to get to know as many people as I possibly could. I was training at the local high school for a power-lifting meet. Tensas Academy was a private school in St. Joseph. As I walking out to my state police car, two Chevy trucks parked behind my unit. One man stepped out. He was tall and large, had long black hair and was wearing cowboy boots, jeans and a tank top. It was obvious to me that he was a serious weight lifter or he just grew up strong. He walked right past me, staring at me all the way. Is this someone I have given a ticket to and don't remember? Man, I hope I don't have to fight this guy. He walked up to me and stuck out his hand.

"Sammy Rogers, sir," he said.

"I'm Bobby Smith, the new state trooper here. It's nice to meet you, sir."

"Don't call me "sir". Call me Sambo."

It's amazing to me that we meet tons of people in our lives, and some times there is no connection, but in others, there is an instant bond. We became great friends and worked out together. He and his family owned a farm, and I began to hang out with them. We talked about farming and I got to be a close member of their family. Three years would pass, and I was enjoying being a state trooper. But that would change.

CHAPTER 8
"HIS BADGE WAS SILVER"
Deputy Don McDuffie
Franklin Parish Sheriff Department

I was working with Bobby at the driver's license checkpoint, and everything was going fine. When suddenly, a small, red car, headed north bound on LA 15, ran through the checkpoint. The car did slow down, but at the last minute, he sped up and almost hit the officers. I was near my unit when I heard the other officer yelling to stop that car. I noticed a trooper getting in his unit and chasing the car in the north bound lane. I jumped in my unit along with Deputy Mike Parker, and we started after them. We began to gain some ground on them when suddenly, the driver of the car slammed on his brakes. The trooper had to drive past the car in order to avoid hitting it. I saw the trooper exit his unit and start toward the car.

I was the K-9 unit for Franklin Parish and had my dog in the back seat. I told Mike, if the violator jumps out and runs, this dog will eat him up in that bean field. Then, the door of the violator's car flew open and a shotgun barrel appeared. At this point, everything went into slow motion. The driver stood up and fired one shot at the trooper. I saw the trooper break for the darkness, and the violator fired a second round. By this time, we had made it to the scene and stopped our unit. We opened the doors and began to get out when the suspect turned and made a gesture as if he were going to shoot us. I fired six rounds. Later I discovered I had hit him four times. Deputy Parker fired one shot and the suspect fell backwards into his car. I told Mike that if he came out with anything else, to kill him.

I ran back to my unit to radio for an ambulance because a trooper had been shot. The other officers had heard the shots and were en route to the scene. The suspect stood and was bleeding profusely from both legs. I told him to turn around and place his hands on the car. He did as he was instructed, then unexpectedly, fell backwards into the highway. As other officers began to arrive and approach the suspect, he was still trying to reach his shotgun that lay only three feet away. We handcuffed him, and it was at that time that I saw that the injured trooper was Bobby.

Everyone was concerned as to whether they should move Bobby or not because of the steady flow of blood from his head and the possibility of a spinal injury. I heard Lt. McDonald ask Bobby if he wanted them to take him to the hospital or if he wanted to wait for the ambulance. Bobby indicated that he wanted his fellow officers to take him to the hospital. Several officers put Bobby in the back of Trooper Shelly Brown's unit. Claudie Sowell was already seated in the back seat. They had placed him in Sowell's lap, positioned much like a child sitting in the lap of his father. They then sped off to the hospital.

We roped off the crime scene and waited for the Crime Lab from Baton Rouge to arrive. As we waited, news came back that the suspect had died and that they were transporting Bobby to the St. Francis Medical Center in Monroe. There were no winners on that particular night. The suspect had lost his life and a fellow officer may also be losing his as well. I was left with the numbing reality that only the grace of God had kept me from suffering such a horrible fate.

During the three-mile trip to Franklin Memorial Hospital, I recalled the incident between the hawk and the rabbit. As we rode, thoughts ran through my head. Is this the day I would die? Is this the day that all police officers process in their mind from time to time?

Only moments earlier I had lay bleeding in the middle of LA 15, but so had the suspect. A distance of only 29 feet separated us. Deputy Joe Curry performed first aid on the suspect by applying bandages and pressure to his heavily bleeding wounds. It seemed ironic that just a moment earlier, the officers were firing at the suspect in an attempt to kill him to protect their own lives, and now they were trying to save him. Their efforts sustained the suspect until the ambulance arrived. The paramedics took over and started their journey to the hospital. One of the bullets fired from my revolver had severed the femoral artery in the suspect's right leg, and one of the bullets from Deputy McDuffie's had severed the femoral artery in his left leg. The officers did everything possible to save the suspect's life, but due to the severity of the severed arteries, the suspect succumbed to his wounds while en route to the hospital.

The hawk was dead.

VISIONS OF COURAGE

CHAPTER 9
CRUCIAL CRITICAL CARE

Trooper Brown backed his unit to the emergency entrance where the nurses and attendants were waiting. They took me out of the unit and placed me on a gurney and rolled me into the emergency room. The nurses began gathering my vital signs and removing my clothes to determine the extent of my injuries.

Trooper Brown, who followed me into the emergency room, began yelling at the nurses and the attending physician, Dr. Greg Tubre. "Don't let Bobby die," he yelled, "Whatever you do, don't let Bobby die!" Due to the escalated emotions he displayed, the nurses tried to remove him from my room, but he refused. I lay there thinking, "Shelly, you need to leave these people alone so they can do their job and save my life." Then the pain began. I began to feel so much terrible pain.

"Bobby, can you hear me?" asked one of the nurses.

"Yes ma'am," I groaned.

"Do you know what your blood type is?" she asked.

"Yes ma'am," I frantically replied. "It's O negative!"

"Bobby, do you understand what I'm asking you," she asked.

"Yes ma'am," I said, "You're asking me what blood type I have. My blood type is O negative."

Doctor Greg Tubre was an attending physician at the Franklin Memorial Hospital. He looked at my injuries and doubted that I would survive. The skin on my face and scalp were peeled back, exposing part of my skull. My left eyelid was also peeled back and damaged, exposing the left eye.

When Dr. Tubre had awoken that morning in New Orleans, he told his wife, Tammy, about a dream that he had had. He remembered that in his dream, there was someone in a uniform, that had been shot and wounded, lying on a dark highway. He couldn't remember much more. Still, this seemed strange to both the doctor and his wife. For some reason this dream made a strong impression on him.

Earlier that Friday evening at about 11 p.m., Doctor Tubre was driving home from New Orleans with his family. He was stopped at the driver's license check point, the same one that the suspect would eventually run through.

Although he rarely stopped at the hospital when he was not working, Dr. Tubre decided to stop. He couldn't explain why he was there, but for whatever reason, he felt compelled to go there. The unusual dream continued to haunt him. This doctor's unexplained urge may very well have kept me alive.

"Please help me," I cried out, "I'm hurt really bad!"

Dr. Tubre almost simultaneously gave me an injection of Demerol. I started to calm down, and unbelievably, my vital signs were close to normal. The doctor still did not know if I was out of danger. The injuries I had incurred were not the type of injuries that this small rural hospital was prepared to handle. By the looks of my wounds, Dr. Tubre believed that some of the pellets from the shotgun blast must have penetrated my brain. Brain damage seemed stronger than just a remote possibility.

Dr. Tubre and his staff did their best to initially treat and stabilize my injuries. However, they were a small county hospital and were not equipped to handle a major head trauma. St. Francis Hospital was the nearest trauma unit, yet it was about a forty mile drive away; but, I had to go there. In fact, I needed to get there real fast.

Dr. Tubre bandaged my bullet riddled face and hands. The bleeding finally stopped. I was in a state of semi-consciousness and murmured incoherently. Dr. Tubre continued to prepare me for a critical and hopefully, quick journey to St. Francis Hospital.

They wheeled me from the emergency room to an ambulance waiting to transport me to Monroe. Trooper Shelly Brown radioed ahead to let the connecting parishes know that the ambulance would be coming through soon. As they placed me in the ambulance, I heard Dr. Tubre talking quietly to the nurse. They were riding in the ambulance with me to monitor my condition.

As we left the hospital, the abrupt accelerations, braking and quick turns made me nauseated. Also, not being able to see had affected my equilibrium, which didn't help matters. I told Dr. Tubre that I was getting sick, and I did. "I'm sorry," I said with a Demerol — influenced apology. At that time, my mind began to wonder again. Was I awake? Was I dreaming? Was I dead?

My vomiting concerned Dr. Tubre. Patients frequently vomit as a result of injury to the brain and that was still a strong concern of the doctors. He couldn't examine my eyes and evaluate how my pupils responded to light. Both of my eyes looked gone. Dr. Tubre just couldn't tell.

I was awakened by the beeping sound of the ambulance backing up to the emergency room entrance of the St. Francis Hospital. I heard a lot of people talking around me as they took me out of the ambulance and wheeled me into the emergency room.

"Bobby, this is Captain Byrd. You're going to be all right," I heard.

Captain Byrd was the commander of Troop F, which was headquartered in Monroe. Captain Byrd was notified of the shooting along with every on-duty and off-duty trooper assigned to Troop F. This was a time to close ranks and have a strong show of support for one of their own.

The closing of ranks involved many more officers than those assigned to Troop F. Police officers from the Monroe Police Department, West Monroe Police Department, and the Ouachita Parish Sheriff's Office were also waiting at the hospital in Monroe for my arrival. Some of my friends were also contacted and were there. There were probably 25 to 30 officers there.

I was so cold lying there in the emergency room. I could hear people around me, and I could feel them working on me, but I was so confused. They gave me some more shots, and I felt like I was going back and forth between consciousness and sleep, between dreaming and reality, possibly between life and death.

All of a sudden I got really scared. I was frantic. I couldn't see anything or hear anything! I felt like I was just lying in bed at night with my eyes closed, and I was listening — listening to the silence. I thought, "Did my soul leave my body? Was this death?" It was so quiet and so still, and I was so afraid. If this was death, it was not going to be a lot of fun and I wasn't ready for it. I couldn't believe how scary this feeling was. I've never been even close to being that scared before. I started screaming for someone to help me. I wanted someone to reassure me that I was alive. But, was I really screaming, or was it merely a thought? Was this all a really bad nightmare? Can you scream if you're dead?

Someone was touching me. That was real. I wasn't dead! I knew that I felt someone touch my hand. A female voice asked, "Bobby, do you know where you are?"

"I'm in the hospital," I replied.

"We are doing all we can for you, but you need to stay calm," the nurse said.

I was still so terrified and was wondering if I was going to live. Again, I was alone in the examining room, and I screamed out from the excruciating pain in my right hand.

VISIONS OF COURAGE

CHAPTER 10
"IT WAS A BEAUTIFUL DAY"
Lt. Jesse Wells
Louisiana State Police

March 14, 1986, is a moment in time that I will never forget. I was working a DWI Task Force Detail in Ouachita Parish. Forty miles away, Trooper Bobby Smith was working a much similar detail in Franklin Parish. I had just arrested a subject for DWI and was transporting him to the Ouachita Parish Jail for booking when the Troop F dispatcher, Jim Dear, advised me that Bobby had been shot. Jim informed me that Bobby's condition was life threatening, and that he was being transported to the Franklin Parish Hospital.

I immediately said a silent prayer for Bobby as I drove to the jail. My eyes filled with tears, and I feared that I would never see him again. Due to the severity of his injuries, I was told that Bobby needed to be transferred to a larger hospital equipped with a trauma facility. It was then that he was transported, by ambulance, to St. Francis Hospital in Monroe, Louisiana.

After my booking was completed, I met the ambulance as it roared into the emergency room at St. Francis. Bobby was quickly removed from the ambulance and wheeled into the emergency room. Even though I had been informed of the severity of his injuries I was still not prepared for what I saw lying on that gurney.

Bobby had suffered a shotgun blast to his face and hands. His scalp was torn away from his skull. The gash seemed to be about two inches long, and it reminded me of an old baseball with worn out threads and the leather separated from the core of the ball.

The doctors on duty began treatment immediately. It was obvious from their actions that they were doing everything possible to save his life. As I stood there, staring at my friend lying there, one of the doctors looked in my direction with a paleness in his face and said in a solemn voice, "You don't get paid enough for this."

As I stood next to Bobby with my hands on his shoulders, I had many thoughts running through my head about him. I remembered the first time I met him. I realized then that he was a man of great character and charisma. He was always willing to help anyone, anytime. As the years went by and our friendship grew, he demonstrated through his actions, that he was a doer and a leader. He had a leadership air about him, and on many different occasions I saw this characteristic demonstrated through his knowledge, confidence, firmness, and fairness. He was a Trooper who could immediately gain control of an accident scene or any other critical situation. Yet, there he was, lying there, fighting for his life.

The doctors finally left the emergency room to confer about Bobby's condition. I heard Bobby scream. Trooper Jimmy Odom and I rushed to his side. Jimmy began rubbing Bobby's feet. Jimmy was a Vietnam veteran who had comforted many of his fallen comrades in such a manner. I was at the head of the gurney talking to Bobby. We were trying to comfort him and encourage him to hold on. As we stood there, Jimmy said a prayer for Bobby.

It was obvious that Bobby was in tremendous pain, and at times, he would lift his ripped, bloody hands in an attempt to touch his face. I remember seeing his biceps bulge and was amazed at how pumped up they were, and wondered what type of adrenaline rush his body was now experiencing.

Only three years earlier, I had been Bobby's Field Training Officer. As I helplessly stood there, I wondered if I could have done anything different years ago that could have prevented this tragedy. But, Bobby was a squared away cadet. He was always alert, conscious of what was going on, and what was happening around him. He also knew the risks. Bobby had good officer survival skills and used them daily. He saw the big picture.

As Jimmy and I tried to comfort Bobby, the seconds seemed like minutes, and the minutes like hours. We were experiencing life in slow motion. During this time, the emergency room crowd of officers continued to grow. It was at times, like these, that we really pulled together.

The doctors finally came back in and took Bobby to surgery. Jimmy and I joined the crowd of friends and officers in the waiting room. Although there was a great crowd of people in this room, there was not a sound being made. Everyone was praying for Bobby. As I sat there in that waiting room, my thoughts turned to Trooper Mike Kees. Mike was a very special friend who had lost his life in the line of duty on February 5, 1983. Mike was with our Heavenly Father but had never been forgotten!

After the accident, I visited Bobby often. It was obvious that he was in a great deal of physical pain and emotional turmoil. At the same time, he never felt sorry for himself and always expressed concern for others. When I visited him, he would always ask what was going on at Troop F and how my day had been going.

I remember that horrible night as if it had happened yesterday. Bobby was a special man, and he could make you feel good just by talking to him. He is sincere about what he says and does. Since the shooting, he continued to demonstrate all those wonderful qualities previously described.

Bobby once told me, shortly after he went home from the hospital, that if his sight ever returned, he would turn every light he could find on, and never turn them off, and never be in the dark again. I don't think any of us realized at the time that he would become a light for the rest of us and keep us out of the dark.

Bobby never gave up and he continued on with his life's work after this grave tragedy. He's a survivor!

CHAPTER 11
"DON'T CRY DADDY"
Terry Smith

My ten-year old daughter, Ashley, saw flashing, red lights in our driveway and came and got me out of bed at about 1 a.m. I walked to the front door half asleep.

As I opened the door, I saw two state troopers and my older brother's wife, Guinell, coming up the sidewalk. I let them in the house. Guinell's eyes were sad, and her head was down. Her lips were quivering when she looked up at me and said, "Bobby's been shot, but he's still alive."

"Oh my God," I replied. "What happened?"

One of the troopers that was with Guinell, Lt. Jim Pease of Troop E, Alexandria, told me what he knew about the shooting. He told me that everyone with the state police was doing everything they could to help. I got dressed and tried to gather myself together the best I could, because I knew that I would have to be the one to tell our dad, Lavon Smith.

The three of us went to our dad's house that was just about a minute away. My stepmother, Edith, answered the door with a very worried look. I could tell that she knew something was wrong. I told her that I had something to tell her, but not to be afraid.

"What's wrong, Terry? Is someone hurt?" she asked.

Mrs. Edith had been a nurse for over 25 years. She had been around other people's sufferings, but it was different when it hit so close to home. She thought of all of us as her own children. Our mom had died on Bobby and Betty's

75

tenth birthday, December 12, 1962. I told her that Bobby had been shot, but he was still alive.

Mrs. Edith wanted to be the one to tell Daddy. By this time, he was awake and had come to the front room where we were all standing. You could see the fear in his eyes when he saw all of us standing there. He immediately started crying when he heard the tragic news. Although he had also worked in hospitals for over thirty years, his experiences had not prepared him for this. He had lost his first wife, and I'm sure he wondered if he would also lose his son.

Daddy and I got in his car, and I drove us from Alexandria to Monroe. Lt. Pease called ahead and let everyone know that we would be coming through, and that we would probably be traveling fast. It didn't take us long to make the 106 mile trip to Monroe, but it seemed to take forever. When we pulled into the parking lot at St. Francis there were police cars everywhere!

We entered the hospital through the emergency room entrance, and they told us that Bobby was in surgery. All we could do was wait. The wait seemed to last forever. As we were waiting, Dr. Raymond Haik, the doctor who had initially operated on Bobby's eyes when he first arrived, approached Daddy and I to inform us of Bobby's condition. The news was not good. He had told us that Bobby's left eye was irreversibly damaged and had to be removed, and that the right eye was severely damaged. The prognosis was extremely dim. Dr. Haik told us that he thought Bobby would never see again.

Never was a long time, a very long time. I felt that cold, sinking, nauseating feeling in the pit of my stomach grow even larger. I sat down with my face in my hands. Then I felt someone touch my shoulder. I turned to see Lt. Bobby Mann looking down at me.

CHAPTER 12
"HE'S MY TWIN BROTHER"
Betty Smith Melenovich

My husband Terry was in the United States Air Force, and we were stationed in Sumter, South Carolina, at Shaw Air Force Base. It was around 5 a.m. when we were awakened by the telephone. It was my stepmother, Edith, with the horrible news that Bobby had been shot in the face. She was very quick to tell me that Bobby was alive. However, if he survived the trauma of the shooting, he would probably never see again. I immediately began crying which woke up my husband, Terry. He knew that something terrible had happened and got up to comfort me.

I hung up the phone and told Terry that Bobby had been shot, and that I had to get to Monroe as quickly as possible. We decided that I would go for now, and that Terry would stay there with our two school-aged children. We made arrangements for me to fly to Monroe that day. All I could do was cry and pray while I packed my bags.

The nearest airport was in Columbia, South Carolina, so as soon as my bags were packed, we headed to the airport with what we thought was plenty of time. When we got to Columbia, there was some sort of festival going on, and most of the streets through town were closed. My time was running short and so was my patience. We stopped several times trying to get directions around the festival, but no one seemed to know any more than we did. Finally, we made it to the airport with only minutes to spare before my flight left. Nothing was going to keep me from getting to my brother.

While I was on the plane, all I could think about was my brother and praying that he would be okay. There were some college students on the plane with me that attended Northeast Louisiana University in Monroe, and they were playing cards. They tried to get me to play with them, but all I could focus on at that time was getting to Monroe as fast as I could.

The plane landed after what seemed like forever. I was met at the airport by two women who I had never met before, and they took me to the hospital. When I got to the hospital, my family was already there and more police officers than I had ever seen before in one place. My brother, Terry, met me as soon as I got to the hospital and took me in to see Bobby. When I walked into Bobby's room, I could not believe how swollen his head was. It was about the size of a basketball. Yet, he was still alive, and that's all I cared about. I told Bobby that I loved him and that I was there if he needed anything. As soon as Terry and I left Bobby's room, I cried. I could not believe what I had just seen. My twin brother lying there looking nothing like himself and so seriously injured.

CHAPTER 13
"TOO MUCH TIME TO THINK"
Danny Smith
Bobby's Oldest Brother

At the time of Bobby's shooting, I was working for Trans World Drilling Company as a safety engineer. About 7:00 a.m. on the morning of March 15, I was working on a stacked rig in the Gulf of Mexico about 100 miles from land. The rig tool pusher received an emergency message for me to call home. As the phone rang, I was anticipating my wife, Guinell, to answer but it was my good friend, Ron Driskall. I said, "Ron, what is going on?" "Bobby's been shot," he said. Being a paramedic and having worked in an emergency room trauma unit, I had seen many gun shot wounds, a lot of which were fatal. My mind was racing, listening to Ron explain to me what happened. Bobby got shot in the head. "How bad is it?" I asked. "We don't know. They just want you to come home as soon as possible," he responded.

I turned to the tool pusher standing next to me and told him I'd have to go home. The chopper is the fastest way back to shore, but none were available this particular day. The only mode of travel which could take me back to my truck, some 100 miles away, was a supply boat. With high winds and waves, it would take me eight or nine hours to get to shore.

I went to my room and began packing my bags, throwing my clothes into a large blue and yellow nylon duffel bag Bobby had given me. It had his name stenciled across the top in bold black letters: Bobby E. Smith.

Lowering me into the boat, we began the long tedious trip back to shore. The crew asked if I wanted to come into the boathouse, but I was in no mood for conversation. As the boat slowly crept towards land, I began pacing back and forth across the deck. My mind raced with unpleasant thoughts about Bobby's condition and seeing him alive again.

The skipper of the boat had tuned in the radio to a Lafayette station in hopes of catching the news, if any, about Bobby's shooting. Eight hours is a long time to think about whether you will ever see your brother alive again. Since the death of our mother some 23 years earlier, and as the oldest child, I had taken on the role as the family protector. But here I was 350 miles away from Bobby, and I felt helpless. As the boat arrived at shore, I grabbed my bag and ran to my truck. I remembered passing Troop I in Lafayette many times on my trip back and forth from my home in Pineville, Louisiana. I turned on the radio and fumbled with the dial trying to find a station that would give a report about the shooting. Troop I was in sight as I pulled from the interstate onto the service road. I walked to the front counter and was greeted by the desk sergeant. "How may I help you?" "I'm Danny Smith. Bobby is my brother who was shot in Monroe last night. Are you aware of his condition?" Other troopers began to walk to the front counter as they overheard the conversation between the sergeant and me.

One trooper picked up the phone saying "I'll call Troop F in Monroe." After a brief conversation, he hung up the phone and turned to me. "Bobby was shot in the head," he said, "but they don't know the full extent of his injuries. They took him to surgery last night, but he is still alive." I thanked them for the information and again proceeded toward home which was an hour and a half away. I finally made it home, pulled into the driveway and our friend, Richard Penual, was waiting. As I stepped from my truck, I asked Richard what was the latest on Bobby? He gave me no additional information. I told him, "I'm going to run into the house, take a quick shower and then we will go."

Intrusive thoughts kept racing through my head. Saddened and grieving, I kept swallowing hard, reminding myself that big boys don't cry. We were back in the truck, and another two hour ride lay ahead of us. Another two hours of wondering what I'd find when we got there. There was little conversation. When Richard and I arrived at the hospital in Monroe, I was amazed by the number of police cars. I took the elevator to the intensive care floor. As the door opened, men and women in police uniforms were everywhere: the state police, the sheriff's office, Monroe and West Monroe Police and other uniforms that I didn't immediately recognize. They were lined down both corridors. I saw Terry, my brother, talking to one of the troopers.

It's around 9 p.m., and for fourteen hours I have asked myself the question, "What shape will I find Bobby in?" My answer came soon. Terry told me Bobby had been shot in the face with a shotgun and had lost one eye. It was uncertain if the remaining eye could be saved. Terry also told me Bobby had been asking for me and wanted to know when I was coming. As I entered the room, Bobby was laughing with some of the family and officers. It's not what you'd expect from someone who had been shot and faced with the possibility of going blind. That wasn't normal behavior, but no one ever accused Bobby of being normal! "Danny, I guess you heard I lost one eye, but I told them to order me a blue eye. That way I could look like a catahoula cur." "Bobby, you truly are sick." Bobby had not had a bath since they brought him in. He told me, "I've been waiting on you to get here, so you can give me a bath."

The next few days could best be described as an emotional roller-coaster. At times, Bobby seemed to be doing extremely well. He laughed and joked about his blindness, and surely since he was blind, he'd be able to play a musical instrument. But his laughter would quickly turn to tears when one of his friends or family members came into the room. It was as if Bobby's emotional state and demeanor was based on the emotional state of those around him. Watching him experience so many emotional changes throughout the day was extremely hard for us.

One particular routine that occurred every morning was becoming more and more frustrating for us. It would happen when Bobby's eye surgeon made his rounds. Bobby had one eye removed, and the remaining eye was beginning to give Bobby more and more problems. The doctor stated that if Bobby continued to have severe pain in his eye, then it would have to be surgically removed. It was an extremely difficult time. Bobby stated that, at this particular time, his greatest fear was to lose his remaining eye, taking away any hope that he would ever see again. It was obvious to us that each morning when the doctor came by, Bobby's attitude would change from happy and positive, to sad and depressed. I had observed this routine for the last time. When the doctor left Bobby's room that day, I followed him down the hall as he walked to the nurses' station.

As the doctor turned around, I said, "I need to talk to you." As a paramedic, I had witnessed some physicians who had a very poor bedside manner, and his doctor had fallen into that category. I told him we were all having a difficult time trying to keep a positive, optimistic attitude about Bobby's progress, and he was making it awfully difficult as a result of his bed side manners. I went on to inform the good doctor that the next time he came into Bobby's room and caused him any more grief, I was going to stomp a mud hole in his butt! I realize this was probably not the appropriate way to handle the situation at hand, but I was speaking from emotions, trying to protect Bobby. The following morning when the doctor came to see Bobby, he apologized to him and the family. From then on, his attitude was optimistic and friendly.

VISIONS OF COURAGE

CHAPTER 14
"BUT...WHY CAN'T I GO?"
Jim Dear

I really don't know where or how to begin, so I will just forego any fancy introductions and say what I have to say.

First of all, I hope no one will be offended by the words I choose to use. It is what I feel, and it is how I'm gonna tell my story, and say what I have to say. If you don't like it, don't read it.

The true test of a person is to put him into a situation where he has to face one of his greatest fears. I'll say, I am not afraid of much but I do have my fears (let Freud figure that one out). As the Communication officer with LSP – I have two fears, aside from something happening to my family. The first being to hit a child with a vehicle, and secondly, to see harm come to a fellow officer. Yes, I consider communication officers to be police officers. If you look at what we do and why we do it, you'll find that there is very little difference between our field and those that actually affect arrests. I know many would choose to disagree with me, but that just shows their stupidity and ignorance. Those that fit this category are invited to add their name to my list, but are probably already there.

As a Louisiana State Police Communication officer, with nearly 22 years of experience in the field, I have had to face this fear only a few times. I thank God for being so merciful. The on-the-job training that we receive does not adequately prepare radio operators to handle these situations. Sure, procedurally we are trained, but never are we even considered when it comes to dealing with the stress involved during and after such an event. For me, there is nothing more stressful than to have an officer get in trouble and ask for help. The limit of a radio operator's ability to help is to send other officers to him. Many things can pass through your mind about what is happening in the time it takes for help to get to him.

I believe this stress is magnified by what is instilled into radio operators incessantly throughout their career. All departments brainwash radio operators into thinking that an officer's safety is their responsibility; this is total crap. If an operator relays all the information he has concerning a situation and the people involved, then he has done all that he can do. How an officer reacts to this information is the key to his safety and survival. I will be the first to admit that a poorly trained, or incompetent radio operator, can quickly and easily get an officer into trouble. Those of us with experience need to be aware and not afraid to speak up when something like this comes to his attention. Sometimes additional training is required, while other times these people must be replaced.

As I said before, a lot can go through an operator's mind from the time that an officer requests assistance until help arrives. But, there have been situations where officers have gotten into trouble with other officers in sight. To me, this is the most stressful situation I have ever experienced. This is because the radio operator has had no part in the events and because of how he has been trained, he still feels responsible. Even though there is absolutely nothing that he can do to change the situation, it doesn't keep him from tearing himself apart by trying to come up with a way to help even though all the help needed is already there.

As I write this, I feel the need to do something to 'undo' all this improper training of radio operators so that no one else has to go through and feel what I have felt in the past. A situation as I have just described happened to me about 12 years ago. Recalling these events are not pleasant at all and stir a lot of emotions that have been pushed back for a long time. Even though I know there was nothing that I could have done differently that would have made any difference, I still feel responsible.

I came to work one night for a 6 p.m. to 6 a.m. shift. All was normal and nothing was happening other than normal shift activities. Sgt. Randy Beckham was working the desk, and Lt. Don McDonald had taken a group of troopers down to Franklin Parish, just south of Winnsboro, to work a DWI check point. The purpose of this check point was to observe a driver's condition while checking their driver's license, insurance, and registration papers. If a person was observed to have been drinking, then appropriate actions would be taken to remove them from behind the wheel.

This check point was being conducted in an area where I did not have direct radio contact with the officers involved, so the radio traffic was being handled by the sheriff's office in Winnsboro. All seemed to be going well until the telephone rang.

Sgt. Beckham took the call and spoke only briefly with the caller, but I could tell from his voice that something was not right. You see, a radio operator quickly becomes trained to the normal, unstressed voice of those he works with and can quickly tell when something is amiss. Sgt. Beckham's voice indicated to me that something was wrong, very wrong.

When Sgt. Beckham had hung up the phone, he immediately turned to me and told me that Lt. McDonald had been shot in the face with a shotgun and was being carried to the hospital there in Winnsboro. Words cannot describe all the thoughts and feelings that went through me at that one moment. One of my greatest fears had reared its ugly head and was staring me straight in the face. I was confused, angry, and sad all at once. But, most of all, I felt totally helpless and useless. I didn't understand how this could have happened with all the officers being present at the check point. I was in shock. I couldn't believe it had happened at all. I wanted to go see for myself. I wanted to go home and not come back. I wanted to cry. I wanted someone to wake me from this nightmare that couldn't be happening.

Minutes seemed like hours. Sgt. Beckham and I were at a loss, we had just been told something that there was no planned reaction for. If you think about it, police work is mostly an action-reaction type job. When some specific event happens, we usually have a planned and well thought out reaction to the event. To this, there was none. We had no information and absolutely nothing to do but wait.

Soon the phone rang again. This time we got more information. And we also learned that it was not Lt. McDonald who had been shot but Trooper Bobby Smith. We were told he had been shot in the face with bird-shot from a fairly close range and was being transported to St. Francis Hospital in Monroe in the back seat of one of the patrol cars. The wait was over. Now we actually had something to do that might be able to possibly help.

The Monroe Police Department was notified and set up to block all traffic lights and intersections while the staff at the hospital's emergency room was notified, and prepared for them to arrive. Needless to say, the 50-mile trip didn't take long, and Bobby was taken into the hospital. I prayed continuously.

Sgt. Beckham and I didn't say a lot to each other. I think we were both too busy with our own thoughts and emotions. I really don't know how it got started, but we started making phone calls. Even though it was after 11p. m., we called and notified everyone that worked out of the troop, to the events that had happened. Even though we did not know anything about Bobby's condition, it was better than just waiting.

At some point during the calls, we received word from the hospital that Bobby's injuries were not life threatening, but he had lost his sight in one eye, and possibly both. I was relieved to learn this, but it still did not help all the thoughts and emotions I was feeling.

It all seems like a blur, and I don't remember much about the remainder of the night except for answering calls asking about Bobby's condition and doing a lot of soul-searching and deciding if I was going to ever come back to work. I didn't know if I wanted to or even if I could. To me, work had turned into something very bad and distasteful. It was something that I just didn't care for anymore.

That morning when I got home, my family was still asleep. As I got undressed and crawled into bed, I didn't know if I could sleep or not. My mind was still spinning from all that had happened. My wife slept on, not even knowing I was there. I couldn't even close my eyes. Mental pictures kept flashing through my mind and eventually my tossing and turning awakened my wife. She took one look at my face and immediately asked me what had happened. That's when the tears started.

I cried for Bobby. I cried for all that had gone wrong. But, as selfish as it may seem, mostly, I cried for me. It has taken time and a lot of thought, but I now realize that there was absolutely nothing that I could have done that would have changed those events. I still blame myself at times, but I get over it. I learned that I have grown from it. But I am still angry and bitter over what happened and the fact that all that I have felt was aggravated because someone decided that the radio operator is responsible.

In the history of the Louisiana State Police, there has only been one radio operator to retire outside of a medical retirement. All of these retired with either heart or blood pressure problems. These problems are now known to be directly related to stress. There are many who quit long before retirement because of the pressures involved. I wish I could change it.

I know what this situation did to me is only minuscule compared to what Bobby went through, or even the officers who were at the scene that witnessed these events. I know that Bobby was the real victim, but was he the only victim?

CHAPTER 15
REALITY REALLY HURTS

It was late that evening after the surgery when I woke up in my hospital room. My wife, Debbie, and my family were there. It was hard to hide the emotional pain. I was the mascot of the family; it had always been easy for me to lighten things up, and there seemed to be no better time than the present. I told my brother, Danny, "You know I've always wanted to play a musical instrument, and I don't know any blind person that can't play a musical instrument and sing. So maybe this will be a good opportunity for me to play my harmonica." My brother, Terry, told me that they were going to buy me a monkey and place me on the sidewalk to sell pencils to make a living since I couldn't be a state trooper anymore. The next fourteen days in the hospital were anything but humorous. There were ups and downs. I tried hard to keep a positive attitude through the numerous surgeries on my eyes, head and hands. I was hopeful that the eye surgeries would be beneficial. Although, in the back of my mind, I knew that the doctor's reports had shown that I would probably never see again. Dr. Raymond Haik had told me that they were forced to remove one of my eyes because of the extensive damage due to the pellets from the shotgun. He said that I still had one eye left, but it was too badly damaged to see through again unless there was divine intervention. Reports like this from the doctor damaged my positive spirit that I was striving so desperately to retain.

While laying there flat on my back, I had a lot of time to think. Someone was in my room with me all the time, but they couldn't tell if I was awake or not, due to the patches that covered my eyes. There were times that I wanted to talk and others when I didn't.

I felt a lot of different feelings. Anger, sorrow, hatred, despair, hope, helplessness and a few other feelings entered my mind. I was having a hard time sorting it all out. I cried often and had a very difficult time keeping my sanity. I really thought that I might be going crazy.

Things began to get a little clearer to me. Flat on my back, the only direction that I could look, was up. I thought there was more above me than just the ceiling over my head. Surely, God must have put me in this position so I would have to look up to Him. I remembered how I ignored God the past few years by not living the life that I had been reared to live. Maybe this was just God's way of slowing me down a little bit in my fast lane life. This had to be a way of God telling me to get my life in His order. I had to slow down and let Him once again be "Lord" of my life.

Many different people came and went in my room. People were always in the halls. One day I overheard some people talking in the hall. I know that they thought that I must have been sleeping when one of them said, "I just wish that he would have died. It would have been so much easier for him, had he just died. Now he's going to be blind, and it's going to be so difficult for Bobby to deal with that." That comment scared me almost as much as when I was first shot.

You never can tell who you may hurt with words. Those words spoken outside my room that day were as if someone had taken a sharp knife and cut deep into my soul. I'm sure that person did not mean to hurt me, but just felt that I would be better off dead than to live my life as a blind person. Often I thought that maybe that person was right.

Sometimes I had various strange thoughts. I wasn't real sure if I was thinking, almost asleep, dreaming or hallucinating from the medication they were giving me for the pain. I wondered if I had brain damage, and if I'd slowly lose my mind. "Was my face grotesquely disfigured? Would I look like a freak and scare little children and others with merely the sight of my face? Would I be permanently blind?" I wondered.

Sometimes I just lay there and cried. I couldn't help but think of why this was happening to me. I knew that people were standing in my room crying. I felt really bad for them. They hurt for me because I was hurting, and I hurt for them because they were hurting. It was a vicious cycle of emotions and helplessness. When I talked, they tried to console me. When they talked, I tried to console them.

I told everyone that visited me that I was okay, knowing deep down inside that I wasn't. They also told me that I would be okay, but deep down inside I knew that I wouldn't be.

Every time I would go to sleep, I would have a nightmare. The nightmares weren't about the shooting but about being harmed. I had been such a self-sufficient person. Now here I was . . . so helpless, so vulnerable, and I was so afraid.

VISIONS OF COURAGE

CHAPTER 16
"IT'S OK FOR COPS TO CRY"
Lt. Bobby Mann
Monroe Police Department

I was sleeping peacefully when the phone awoke me at 2 a.m. It was Jimmy Zambie with the Monroe Police Department. His voice was very solemn. He told me that Bobby had been shot and was in St. Francis Hospital. "What happened?" I asked. Jimmy was not sure of all the details, but he said that Bobby had made a traffic stop on Hwy. 15 out of Winnsboro, and the guy shot him.

I got out of bed, dressed and headed to the hospital. On the way, I began to think about my friendship with Bobby. As I drove, my mind went back to when I first met him.

Bobby started working at the Monroe Police Department in 1975. He was a typical rookie — young, good looking, and full of energy. You couldn't help but like him from the first time you met him. He was funny, easy going, and was always pulling pranks on people. But, the most important thing about Bobby was that he had a lot of common sense. We worked together on the night shift for several years. Bobby left the police department in 1983 to fulfill his life's dream of becoming a Louisiana State Trooper. He was there for me when I went through my divorce. As a police officer, Bobby too, had also gone through a divorce and knew firsthand what I had experienced.

When I arrived at the hospital, there were so many people there, but no one knew exactly what had happened. I walked around, talking with different people, trying to get an answer to "WHY?" I saw Bobby's brother, Terry, from Alexandria, and I walked over to him. Jackie Coleman, Bobby's partner, was also there, and I guess Jackie knew more about the shooting than anyone else. The only positive thing I could find out was that the guy who shot Bobby had been killed. That was not the Christian thing to think, but a cop develops a hard case attitude, especially when another cop and friend has been shot.

Unable to see Bobby, I left the hospital about 5 a.m. I went home and my wife, Monica, was up waiting for some news. Monica and I sat at the kitchen table and talked about when Bobby and I lived together at the Spanish Villa Apartments, as did Monica and her roommate. We both cried and held each other in an effort to console one another. Later, that same morning, I went back to the hospital. I spoke with Debbie, Bobby's wife, and Jackie Coleman. Jackie was able to get me into ICU to see Bobby. As I walked in, I saw him with his eyes and hands bandaged. Jackie told Bobby that it was me, but he didn't know who I was at that time. I asked Bobby how he felt. He responded with a chuckle, "OK." I told him that this was a heck of a way to get transferred back to Monroe, and he laughed out loud. Debbie was standing at the door of his room crying. I told Bobby to hang in there, and if he needed anything, that I would be right outside. I left his room with tears in my eyes. You have to understand, a cop isn't expected to show emotions, but I did.

CHAPTER 17
"WHY DO I FEEL SO GUILTY?"
Trooper Mike Epps
Louisiana State Police

I first met Bobby when I was with the Ouachita Parish Sheriff's Office. I was going to execute an arrest warrant off of Washington Street in Monroe. I requested someone from Monroe PD to come with me, and they sent Bobby. If I had only known what the future held, I would probably have run off, screaming down Washington Street. Well, I didn't, and we ended up locking this guy up. I could remember running into him periodically while patrolling, but we had nothing other than occasional talks in parking lots while we were on duty. As time went on, we began running into each other more often. When Bobby started working narcotics for West Monroe PD, we would meet on warrants issued, drug round-ups, and downtown at the jail. I resigned from the Sheriff's Office and went to work with the State Police. It was not until Bobby decided that he wanted to become a State Trooper that I really got to know him. Bobby and Jackie were both hired by the State Police and went to the academy together. I remember when they got out of the academy and were assigned together to Tensas Parish. Then we started really spending a lot of time together.

About two years after they were assigned to Tensas Parish, Jackie was reassigned to Ouachita Parish to do Criminal Patrol. Even after he left Tensas Parish, we still seemed to run into Bobby at the troop.

Shortly after Criminal Patrols came into existence, I

came up with the notion that driver's license checks at night would be a good idea, especially if it was done at the right location – like an exit ramp. Naturally, I was thinking about how many drug traffickers I could put in jail. I ran it by Jackie, and he thought it was a good idea too, so we gave it a try. One night Bobby was in Ouachita Parish, and he met Jackie and I at one of the exit ramps to help us. It went great! At one point, Bobby had three people arrested in his car. I had three in my car, and we had some potential arrests sitting on the roadside.

Jackie and I had just gotten back from a Criminal Patrol school on a Friday. I had been asleep for a couple of hours; it was around midnight when Jackie called.

"Bobby's been shot," he said.

"How bad?"

"Pretty bad."

"Where did he get hit?"

"In the head."

I had seen enough head wounds to know that Bobby would either die or at a minimum, suffer extensive brain damage. At that point, my body went numb with shock.

I asked Jackie where Bobby was, and he said they were bringing him to Monroe. I then asked what had happened to the guy that shot Bobby and Jackie told me that he had been shot and he thought he was dead.

I sat on the edge of my bed with my head hung down. My wife, Annette, asked what was wrong. I told her that Bobby had been shot, and it didn't look good. I laid back down but couldn't go back to sleep for a long time. I debated getting dressed and going to the hospital, but I just laid there, starring into the darkness until I finally dozed off. About 6 a.m., Jay Jordan called to tell me about Bobby's shooting. I told him that I already knew and hung the phone up. I didn't ask any details; I just hung up on him.

I got out of bed after that and went downtown. I ran into Mike Wheelis and Rob Fowler, and they began asking me about it.

I called the hospital several times the first day, to check on Bobby's progress. I didn't go to the hospital that first day, because I didn't want to face it. I found out that Bobby had been shot during a nighttime driver's license check. That is when it hit me. I was responsible for the incident. When I first thought about doing night time driver's license checks, I knew it would be dangerous, but the macho came out in me, and I just knew I could handle it. We did a few nighttime checks and everything went fine, so I convinced myself that I was just paranoid and that it wasn't any more dangerous than anything else we had to do. Lt. McDonald felt guilty, but it wasn't his idea, so it wasn't his fault. It wasn't Jackie's idea; it wasn't his fault. It was my idea, and it was my fault. I was wrong, and it was Bobby who paid the price, not me. I suffer with that thought to this day.

I didn't go to the hospital to see Bobby for at least three or four days because I couldn't stand to see the pain and suffering he was going through without blaming myself.

When I walked into the hospital room on my first visit, I saw that Bobby's head and hands were heavily bandaged. As I spent time in his room, the one thing that overwhelmed me more than anything else was the insecurity that Bobby had about not being able to see. He had always been so energetic and outgoing, but the change I saw really shocked me. One day I was standing next to Bobby's bed and he whispered to me, "Who's in here?" I named off everyone that was there in his room. When someone would open the door, he would want to know who came in.

During Bobby's stay in the hospital, the other Criminal Patrol Officer, Charlie Heard, was off, and it was just Jackie and I on patrol. It became evident very quickly that Jackie was having trouble keeping his mind on the patrol, so I told him to just stay at the hospital with Bobby and I would take care of the shifts. I was really worried about Jackie; he took the shooting very hard, but for different reasons than I.

One night, while Bobby was in the hospital I had a traffic stop on Interstate 20 in West Monroe. I asked the guy to step out of the car, and he refused. I saw him reaching under the seat, and I called over the P.A. system for him to get out of the car. I saw him looking in the rearview mirror, but he still didn't get out of the car. I called the troop and told them what had happened. It was like God started dropping police cars out of the sky. I don't know where they came from, but in a matter of minutes, there were cars from the State Police, West Monroe PD and the Sheriff's Office blocking the whole lane of the Interstate. I had to extricate the man from the car, and he and I were both impressed by the show of force. When the smoke cleared, the man promised that he would do exactly what I said. Judging by that kind of response from the other units, it was evident that Bobby's shooting was still very fresh on everyone's mind.

CHAPTER 18
SPIDERMAN WOULD HAVE
BEEN PROUD

Terry was staying with me during this particular night. Because of the pain medication and the emotional state I was in, I would sometimes go into a rage and pull the IV's from my arm and tear the bandages from my face and hands. Therefore, it was necessary for someone to stay with me 24 hours a day. I awoke quite confused and in a sweat. I knew I was in a bed, but not really sure of my location. I sat up, which disturbed Terry who had his feet propped on the end of my bed. He asked me what I was doing.

"Who are you?" I asked.

"Bobby, it's me, Terry," he replied. "What is wrong?"

"Why are you holding me here?" I asked.

"Holding you where?" he asked.

"Holding me here, in this concentration camp," I stated.

Terry tried to reassure me that I was in the hospital. He asked me if I remembered what had happened to me. I wasn't sure. He began to tell me about the shooting to try and jog my memory. He was trying to bring me back from wherever I was. I did not remember anything that he was talking about. In my mind, all I knew was that they were holding me, against my will, in a concentration camp and I wanted out! I started trying to get out of bed. Terry tried to restrain and console me. I stood up and pulled the IV's from my arms. Then I tore the bandages from my face and hands.

I could feel the pain run through my hands as I jumped from the bed landing on my hands and feet. I had become Spiderman! Terry pressed the nurse's button to get help. He continued to console me and try to get me back into bed.

"No," I shouted. "I'm getting out of here, you can't hold me against my will!"

I could still feel the pain running up my arms from landing on my hands and feet on the cold, hard floor. Needless to say, everything was very confusing. Right was left, and in was out. Nothing made any sense! Although I was blind, supposedly living in a world of total darkness, I could see colors. The room was yellow and black checked, like a checkerboard. A nurse came running in the room, but I thought she was rushing out. The nurse tried to convince me to get back in the bed, but I refused.

"Get away from me," I growled at her, " I have done nothing to deserve this treatment!"

She told me that I was hallucinating. I refused to believe her, and still wanted out.

"If you are my nurse, what is your name?" I asked her. She told me her name, but I still remained suspicious because I could not remember meeting her before. I just wanted someone or something familiar. Although I knew who Terry was, I felt that he, like the nurse, was a part of the conspiracy to hold me captive.

Then I asked them where the rest of my family was. Terry assured me that he would call them, and they would come if I would get back into the bed. Then, I told him I wanted to talk to Jimmy Odom. We had been officers together and friends for a long time. I knew that he would not lie to me. I reached for the phone and tried to dial.

"Who are you going to call?" Terry asked.

"I'm calling Jimmy," I replied. "I know he won't lie

to me."

I could not dial the phone because there were still some bandages left on my hands. Terry dialed the troop, and Sgt. Jesse Wells answered the phone.

"Jesse, this is Bobby," I said.

"How are you doing, Bobby?" he asked.

"I'm not doing well at all," I answered. "They are holding me in this concentration camp, and I need somebody to come get me. I need Jimmy to come get me out of here and tell me what is going on."

Jesse went to another phone to call Jimmy. As I waited, I wondered if maybe Jesse was in on this ploy, too. "Were they trying to kill me? What was going on?" Sgt. Wells came back to the phone and told me that he had gotten in touch with Jimmy and that Jimmy was on his way. Jimmy lived 30 miles from the hospital, so it would be a little while before he arrived. Sgt. Wells offered to come and be with me until Jimmy got there. I told him that I didn't care. I just needed Jimmy.

Finally, Jimmy arrived. He came over to where I was sitting on the floor, in the bathroom, next to the toilet, and sat down beside me and hugged my neck.

"Hey, man, I understand you're having a little problem," he said. "Would you like to tell me about it?"

"They are holding me here in this concentration camp, and I just want to go home," I told him.

He reassured me that I was not in a concentration camp and tried to jog my memory of the shooting. I was so confused, because I did not remember the shooting. After listening intently to Jimmy, I began to sob uncontrollably as the pieces of my memories began to fall together. I felt comforted from Jimmy's presence, but most of all, I trusted him. I knew he wouldn't lie to me.

103

A few minutes later, my neurosurgeon, Dr. Greer, came in my room. He, too, came over and took a seat on the bathroom floor beside me. He asked me if he could look at my wounds to see if I had done any further damage to them. I hadn't, but he told me he needed to replace my bandages.

They helped me back into the bed, and Dr. Greer replaced all of the bandages. A nurse came in and gave me something for the pain.

Still sobbing, I asked Dr. Greer if I was losing my mind. He assured me that I would be okay. It would just take some time.

CHAPTER 19
IN SEARCH FOR HOPE

The next morning, my ophthalmologist, Dr. Raymond Haik, came by for his morning visit. He was very direct with me. He knew about the severe pain that I had been having in my right eye and told me that if the headaches didn't go away, that they would have to remove my right eye. That was my greatest fear. If I could keep my eye, there was still a glimmer of hope that maybe one day I could see again. If they took my eye, I had no hope.

Dr. Haik told me about an eye specialist in Memphis, Tennessee, and asked if I would object to him making arrangements for me to see him. I told him I would do anything that might bring my sight back. There was my hope! I finally had something that I could hold on to! Maybe this would be the doctor that would bring my sight back. It was all I had and I was clinging to it! I was on my way to Memphis.

VISIONS OF COURAGE

CHAPTER 20
"YOU'RE WEARING ME OUT!"
Lt. Bobby Mann
Monroe Police Department

The night before Bobby was to leave for Memphis, Debbie asked me if I would stay the night with Bobby, so she could go home and pack. Bobby was in a tremendous amount of pain; however, Bobby was used to pain. We used to lift weights at the YMCA. I had seen Bobby lift through pain, but this was different.

There were places on his scalp where the shotgun pellets had hit. These wounds had scabbed over, therefore causing a lot of itching. During the night, Bobby would unconsciously pick at them. I spent the entire night scolding him for picking at his scabs.

At one point during the night, Pat Stewart with the Monroe Police Department, came in to visit. Bobby had been wanting to take a shower, so I told him since Pat was there and could help me, that I would let him take a shower. We got Bobby into the shower, and to my surprise he was sleep-walking. Bobby began to tell us that he could see. Bobby was talking crazy. Pat was a Vietnam veteran, and as a result of that, he was a little jumpy. I first had to calm Pat and then we got Bobby out of the shower. We dried Bobby, put his PJ's on him and put him to bed. After he dropped off to sleep, Pat peeled out of there. Bobby was in and out all night long and talking out of his head. When morning finally came, I was worn out.

I thought this would be a new beginning. It was Wednesday, March 26, 1986. There it was, just twelve days since my shooting, and I was getting ready to leave the hospital. I not only wanted to see again, I had to. I was a little apprehensive about going to Memphis, but I knew it was my only chance. New journeys were always exciting to me when I could see, but now I wasn't so sure of this seemingly different world outside my hospital room.

I wanted to look good when I left the hospital. I remembered seeing some students from Ruston, Louisiana's blind school, once while I was driving through as a State Trooper. I saw them walking with their canes, yet I still wondered why their clothes looked so mismatched. I thought that just because they were blind didn't mean that they had an excuse to dress so terribly. Therefore, I wanted to be certain I looked good when I went into the visual world the next day.

While I was in the hospital, I had received numerous cards, letters and flowers from friends, fellow officers and even people I didn't know. When I was getting ready to leave, I asked the nurse if she would give my flowers to others in the hospital that maybe hadn't received any because there were too many for us to take home. However, I made sure that I took every card and letter with me to Memphis.

It was finally time to go. A nurse came, and I sat in a wheelchair. She wheeled me downstairs and outside where Trooper Mike Epps was waiting, in his unit, to take me to the airport. As she stopped the chair, at the car, I stood up. It felt great to be outside and smell fresh air. The air smelled so good that I wanted to taste it. I opened my mouth and tried to taste it. I had never tasted air before, nor did I ever have the urge to do so, but this time I was glad that I could.

The wind blew on my face. I was always an outdoorsman; yet, I had never really noticed how the wind felt on my face. I felt like nature was blowing me a kiss. I loved nature, and here she was, returning that love to me.

Mike was a good friend of mine. We had worked together before when I worked at the Monroe Police Department and he worked at the Ouachita Parish Sheriff's Department. Then, we both worked for the Louisiana State Police. He tried to help me in the car. This was the first time I had been in a vehicle since my shooting. I always had a tendency to get car sick before, and being blind did not help matters! It felt really strange when the car started moving. I had never felt like that before, and it didn't feel right. We only got a few blocks away, and I got sick to my stomach. I told Mike, "Stop the car now!" and he did. The trip to the airport took a lot longer than it should have. Even though he was driving slowly, I still had to stop every couple of minutes and throw up. I was real embarrassed and kept apologizing. He kept telling me not to worry about it. I felt like the little kid that keeps on having to go to the bathroom when you're on a long trip.

The plane was waiting for us when we got to the Monroe Regional Airport. The news media was there, and they were talking to me about my injury. I told them that I thought my chances of recovering my sight were real good and that I felt great. I told them that if there was even a slim chance that I would see again and that if my eye wasn't completely damaged, I knew that I would see again. I told them that the doctor in Memphis was the best in the world, and that he would restore my sight. I thanked them and told them that I would see them later. A lady's voice came from the crowd, and she said, "We know you will, Bobby, good luck."

Mr. James Davison was a prominent businessman

from Ruston. He had always been a big supporter of law enforcement. When he heard of my incident, he called the troop and offered to help. He knew from the news articles that I would be traveling to Memphis for surgery. He called and offered to fly my family and me on his company jet at no expense to us.

My wife Debbie, my brothers, Danny and Terry, Greg Gossler, Jerry Mayfield, Randy Beckham and Mike Epps all flew with me to Memphis. We felt pretty good during the flight, and I didn't get sick on the plane. The mood was extremely good. My wife and some of my friends and relatives were going with me to the place where I would get my sight restored. The trip seemed to last only a short time.

When we landed in Memphis, we were met by Trooper Ron Scammerhorn of the Tennessee State Police. He was officially assigned to us during our stay in Memphis. I felt that he was tall and thin when I shook his hand. I knew that he was a good ole country boy by the way his voice sounded. He told me that I was to get anything that I needed from him and the Tennessee State Police.

Ron Scammerhorn was the first personal friend I made since I had been shot. I had gotten to know a few other people when I was in the hospital, and I liked them, but we never developed a personal friendship. Ron and I had much in common: we were both state troopers, and we were both good ole country boys that enjoyed farming. He couldn't do enough for me. I just knew he was going to be a lifelong friend.

I rode in the front seat of Ron's police unit and my two brothers rode in the back seat. I joked with Danny and Terry. I told them that they were probably accustomed to riding in the back seat of a police unit. The rest of my group rode in another car, courtesy of the Tennessee State Police.

I noticed that the Tennessee State Police vehicles were set up a little different from our state police units. I feared that I might get car sick again, but for whatever reason, I didn't during this 30 minute ride from the airport to the doctor's office. As far as I was concerned, we couldn't drive fast enough.

We walked into the doctor's office for my first examination. Danny told the receptionist that we were there to see Dr. Steven Charles.

I heard some of the ladies that worked there ask who I was. One lady said she thought I was a professional football player. I was wearing a pair of gray coaching shorts and a black Oakland Raiders T-shirt. I had been training heavily for an upcoming power lifting competition, and I looked pretty strong and bowed up.

There were people there from Saudi Arabia, Colorado, and other parts of the country. This was when I realized that Dr. Haik was right, this man really must have been the best in the world.

Dr. Charles came out to meet me and shook my hand. He had a good, firm handshake. I liked that. He told me to take his arm, and he walked me to his office. He helped me sit down. He did so in such a way that it really didn't feel like he helped me at all.

He told me that he wasn't going to lie to me or give me false hope, and that there was extensive damage to my remaining eye. He also told me that I would probably never see again. He said they were going to do surgery, but that it was mostly for cosmetic reasons, so my eye would look natural. He then told me the words that I longed to hear, there was a possibility that I could see again. I knew it was a slim chance, but it was a chance.

I really liked Dr. Charles. He spent some time just

talking with me. He told me that he was an avid exercise enthusiast and that he could tell from reading my medical records that I also liked to participate in physical fitness. He told me that my good physical and mental condition was probably what saved my life.

I was told to check into the hospital that night and was scheduled for surgery the next morning at 6:30. I checked in and had a real tough time falling asleep. I woke up a couple of hours before the surgery and was trying to mentally prepare myself. I was getting very nervous. I became so nervous that it turned into panic. The nurse came by to let me know that she would be back soon to give me a shot to prepare me for surgery. I told her that I didn't think that I could wait. I asked her if she would please give it to me now. I was just about to become hysterical when she came back with my shot. I began to pray, "Lord, please let the shot work quickly." Panic had overwhelmed my body and thoughts of the surgery and all the possibilities were racing through my head.

When the nurse wheeled me down the hall to the operating room, my shot still hadn't taken affect. There was a man there wearing a surgical mask. He was the anesthesiologist. I asked him to please hurry because I didn't think I could stand it any longer know I am really losing my mind.

All of a sudden, I felt the anesthetic as it went into my arm. It felt like ice cubes were running through my veins. It was such a relief! I could feel my brain starting to cool down. At any second, the anesthetic would numb my brain and then I would be unconscious. I knew that when I was unconscious I wouldn't have the gripping fear and anxiety any longer. What a relief!

The next thing I remembered was waking up in the recovery room. As I lay in that cold room, I prayed, " God, please let me be able to see when they take these bandages off."

Soon the nurses came and took me back to my room. They must have given me some medication to relax me after the surgery because I fell asleep. While I was asleep, I dreamed about being a policeman. I made a traffic stop. I thought to myself, "Hey, wait a minute! I'm blind! I can't be a cop anymore. Of course, I can be a cop, I'm seeing now so I must not be blind anymore." That dream confused me so much because it seemed so real.

Dr. Charles came into the room as I was waking up. He told me that he was going to remove the bandages. I was excited and scared, all at once. He removed the bandages. Once again I prayed, "Please, God, let me see." I opened my eyes. I couldn't believe it: there was nothing but total darkness.

Panic ran wildly throughout my body. I guess Dr. Charles could sense my panic and shock. He told me that there was a lot of blood, so even if the surgery had been successful, I probably couldn't see right now. It would take a few days to clear up. I was relieved to hear that. There was still a sliver of hope glimmering in the distance. I still believed.

I stayed in the hospital for two more days. The time seemed to take forever to pass, as I anticipated regaining my sight. Seconds seemed like hours and hours seemed like eternities. I no longer had those bothersome bandages on my eyes. I kept waiting to see the light.

Three days passed, and I never saw the light that I had been so eagerly anticipating. It was time to go home and face the bleak reality.

VISIONS OF COURAGE

CHAPTER 21
GOING HOME

I checked out of the hospital and boarded the plane home. As we made the journey, I hoped that the news media was unaware of my return. I couldn't face those people I had so proudly boasted to days before, that I would "see" when I returned. Debbie and I drove home from the airport. That short trip seemed to last forever. As she drove, I wondered if I was prepared for this. She pulled the car under the carport, and we walked through the door and sat on the couch.

It was the first time I had walked into my house blind. It was the first time I had never been able to see my cherished, familiar surroundings. I began to cry. I rose from the couch to go to the bathroom. I had forgotten about the coffee table that was in the middle of the room. The coffee table hit me about mid shin. I had hit so hard that blood rolled down my legs. I knew then that this was going to be a tough time for me. I continued to try to make my way across the living room to the hallway, and down the hall to the bathroom.

As I stood over the toilet, I wondered, "How do you do this?" I had never thought about that before. "How do you use a toilet if you can't see it?" To be safe, I turned around and sat on the toilet. As I sat there, I really began to sob. This was not fair; it's just not fair! As I left the bathroom, I stepped into the hall. I sat down and leaned against the wall. I wondered how long would it take me to learn to move from one room to another without running over things. I heard Debbie coming from down the hall. She sat down beside me, and we held each other and cried. This would become a very common event.

Later that evening, Debbie pulled out the letters and cards I had gotten, in an attempt to make me feel better.

"Do you want me to read some of them to you?" she asked.

"It doesn't matter," I said, "It won't bring my sight back."

"It might make you feel better," she consoled.

There were letters from my friends, the guys I worked with at the troop, and police officers from other agencies. There were also some from people I didn't even know.

One card read:

"Dear Trooper Smith,

I know you don't remember me. You stopped me about a year and a half ago in Tensas Parish on Hwy. 65. I heard about you being shot, and I was touched tremendously. I recalled how polite and courteous you were to me on that stop. You told me to slow down, put my seat belt on, and have a good day. I pray that one day you will receive your sight again and you can go back to work. We'll miss you."

These words, although they were meant to be words of encouragement, only made me sadder, knowing that I would never be able to do that job again.

I was glad that I was home, and it felt good. Debbie and I had talked about our marriage at the hospital in Monroe. We both had our problems, and our marriage was floundering before I got shot. Our problems were compounded by a current problem of great magnitude: my blindness!

It was necessary for us to get in touch with our feelings. We talked about the differences in our relationship and where we stood with each other. We agreed that maybe this was God's way of trying to get us to change our lives and begin to love each other like He knew we should.

We said that we would try our best to make the marriage work. I loved her, and now I needed her love more than ever. I asked her to please be there for me. She told me that she would do her best.

It was my first night back in my own bed. I tossed and turned for what seemed to be all night. I finally took some medication to help me sleep. But sleep did not come, only nightmares and flashbacks. I wrestled with feelings of fear, anxiety and reminders of the horror that I had gone through. This was the beginning of many restless nights. There was no peaceful sleep. There were only nightmares, flashbacks, and cold sweats. I knew that I was going down, both physically and mentally.

My friends and colleagues visited me every day. There was always someone to take me walking, talk with, or to just cry with me. After several weeks at home, I developed agoraphobia, the fear of going outside. I thought my only safe place was my couch with the phone right beside me and the TV remote control in my hand. I didn't want to go back to the bedroom anymore. That was where the nightmares and flashbacks were lurking, waiting for a chance to attack me during a vulnerable moment.

Troopers would also come by to visit. Since I had always been the prankster, I tried to make them feel at ease. I joked around like everything was going to be okay. On the outside, everything was fine, but on the inside, there was a volcano brewing that threatened to erupt at any second. I was trying to hold it back. I didn't want my friends to feel uncomfortable. I knew they were probably hurting emotionally as much as I. Many wanted to help me, but didn't know what to do. Many wished they could give me my sight back, but there was no way. The feelings of helplessness were tremendous. As soon as they would leave, I would go straight to my room, curl up in the corner and have an anxiety attack. I wept, uncontrollably, for hours at a time. I prayed that God would make it stop.

"Where is my comfort and peace, God?" I wondered. "You always said that if we would call upon you, you would give us peace. Where was my peace? Where was my comfort?"

As I sat there, I thought of a poem my daughter, Kim, had given me while I was in the hospital. The title of the poem was "Footprints in the Sand." It told about a man walking along the beach. When he looked back over the path of his life, he noticed that there were always two sets of footprints in the sand. One set was his and the other was God's. He noticed that through the tough times in his life that there was only one set of footprints. He questioned the Lord about this. He asked Him where He went during the hard times. Now I was wondering this same thing. "Where was God?" I really needed Him now. Then God told the man that He loved him so much and that He would never, NEVER leave him. God told him that during those hard times, when there was only one set of footprints, He was carrying him. That poem helped me begin to understand God's role during my suffering. Whoever wrote that poem had no idea of the impact it was to have on my life and surely, countless others.

One night a local DJ gave me a call. He asked me if I was going to be home in the morning at 9:00. I assured him that I would be there, just like I was every day. He told me to listen to his station at 9:00 the next morning. He wanted me to listen to a show called *Electric Dedications* where people would call in and make a song dedication to someone.

That night I took my sleeping pills so I could get a

good night's rest and be ready for the show the next morning. I felt like a child on Christmas Eve night. I was excited and didn't have any idea of what surprise that may have been in store for me. The next morning I was up ready. All of a sudden I heard Trooper Shelly Brown's voice come over the radio. He began telling my story. He talked about what had happened to me only four weeks earlier. He told of how I was blinded in the line of duty, and would probably be blind the rest of my life. He went on to say that the State Police and the local police agencies were making this dedication to me. As I sat there with eager anticipation, I heard the song begin. It was Lee Greenwood singing "God Bless the USA." I sat there and listened intently to the words of that song. Tears began rolling down my face because I was a patriot. I believed in America, and I was a freedom fighter. We officers were freedom fighters, and it broke my heart to know that I would never be able to put that uniform on again. I never forgot that special dedication and caught myself listening to the radio even more. From then on, every time I heard that song, tears would automatically flow from my eyes.

After about a month, it was time for Debbie to go back to work at the bank. This was extremely difficult for me because I had the fear of being left alone, but I knew that she needed a break. She needed to get away and continue with her normal life Each evening she would come home, cook supper, and try to provide the emotional support I needed. But she didn't have much to give. The shooting had left her too emotionally bankrupt.

We tried to get out in the evenings and go for walks to get some exercise; but, mainly to get out of the house. These walks were always interrupted by anxiety attacks that came when I left the house. We would have to rush back to my security blanket, the couch. Many nights I sat on that couch and I could hear Debbie in the bedroom sobbing. I wondered when this would all go away. I wondered if we would ever be able to live a normal life again.

CHAPTER 22
"I'VE GOTTA GO HOME"
Betty Smith Melenovich

During the weeks after Bobby's surgery, after I had left, I could not think of anything but of how alone Bobby must have been feeling. I knew Debbie had gone back to work and I also knew Bobby was having such a difficult time dealing with his new world. As soon as we got back home, Terry and I began trying to get transferred to England Air Force Base in Alexandria, Louisiana, so we could be closer to Bobby. We were unable to get transferred there; but were able to get transferred to Barksdale Air Force Base in Shreveport, Louisiana, which was only about two hours from Monroe.

As soon as school was out, the girls and I moved back to our home in Alexandria. That is where all of our family lived, and they could help with the girls while I tried to take care of Bobby. Terry would come home on the weekends, so I would spend most of the week in Monroe. It seemed like I spent an awful lot of time in Monroe, but Bobby was just not doing well emotionally.

It was becoming obvious that Bobby and Debbie were not only struggling with his injury but were struggling in their marriage as well. We felt that Debbie was not spending enough time with Bobby. It was only a short time later that they were separated and she moved into an apartment. After she left, the family pleaded with Bobby to get him to move home to Alexandria, but he would not. Mostly because Kim was living in West Monroe, and he wanted to be near her.

VISIONS OF COURAGE

CHAPTER 23
BACK TO MY ROOTS

I was born and reared in a devout Christian home. I was born on December 12, 1952, along with my twin sister, Betty. My dad, Lavon, and my mom, Alma, already had two children. Danny was the oldest, and Terry was after him. We were a very close-knit family. We didn't have much money, but we made up for it in love.

My dad worked at the hospital many years after he had gotten out of the service. My mom worked periodically outside the home but developed a severe, fatal disease. She died on my birthday in 1962.

I remembered so many things my mom and dad taught us before her death. Things like, *"The Lord won't put more on you than you can handle."* After my shooting, during my time of healing, I talked to her many times out loud, as if she were right there with me. I wanted her to explain that saying to me, because some days it would seem like my load was too heavy for me to carry.

I reminisced about the times my mom would read us Bible stories at night and the trips we made to church every Sunday. Those were things that were very important to Mom and Dad.

There was a Bible verse that had been brought to my mind several times in the last few years. "Train up a child in the way that he would go, and when he is old he will not depart from those ways." Proverbs 22:6.

After I had become an adult, I had moved away from my home church and had quit going completely. My state police unit F-18 had become my temple. I was serving the people and the Louisiana State Police Department in place of God. A few months prior to my shooting I had been deeply conflicted about my lack of commitment to God. Was I really serving God? Was I doing the things that I was supposed to, to serve Him? Was I serving my fellow man more than God? I felt that I had failed miserably as a Christian.

It often amuses me how we seem to put God in a bottle and conveniently place him on a shelf until we need Him. When things get rough, we take God off of our shelf, only to place him there again when we are through using Him.

I recalled when I had lain face down on LA 15. While the blood was running down my face, I wished I could get my hands on that bottle because I was in desperate need of God. I began to plead with God while I was struggling to sustain my life.

"God, if you will give me one more chance I will serve you," I offered. "If you will get me out of this valley, I will do right."

I thought about all the broken promises I had made to God. I firmly believe that at the time of death there is a battle between good and evil for your soul. I felt that battle. There was a cold, raspy voice on one side that said, "Go ahead and die. There is no way you will live. Why are you calling on your God? Do you think you deserve *His* audience? He won't listen to you." There was a gentle voice that told me just the opposite, "Bobby, you are going to be okay." All of this was very confusing to me. I was afraid to die. I knew that I had turned my back on God for many years and began serving myself. Still, I begged God to not let me die. I was not prepared for death and I sure did not want to spend eternity in hell.

124

"Please give me a second chance, don't let me die," I begged God.

There I was, like so many others, trying to take God off my shelf at my convenience. I desperately needed His help with this situation. So, I took him down and let Him out of that bottle.

"Okay God, if you are there and if you are real, I need your help," I prayed. "I've lost my career, sight, desire to live, and my marriage is in turmoil. Where else can I go?"

I called John, a friend of mine, who went to church just down the street at North Monroe Baptist Church. He was a former Monroe Police Officer. We had worked together for several years. He was involved in the Single's Ministry at North Monroe. He, too, had traveled some of the roads I had traveled. I knew he would understand how I felt.

That Saturday evening, I picked up the phone and dialed John's number. I asked him if he was going to church the next day, and he said sure. I asked him if he would pick me up for church, and he assured me that he would. The next morning, I got out of bed and began getting dressed. I was uneasy. I feared the agoraphobia would kick in when I left for church. But I knew that if there was any one place I needed to be, it was at church, around Christian people who loved one another.

The choir began singing as I sat in the church. That strong feeling of conviction once again came over me. I began sweating profusely and trembling violently with a panic attack. I wanted to stand up, but I felt that I could not. John noticed my uneasiness. We got up and started to leave the church. I knew everyone must have been staring at us. Those relentless tears began rolling down my face, once again. When we got outside, I sat down on the church's steps, placed my head in my hands and sobbed, unable to control it. I wanted to run away, but I couldn't. John sat down next to me and tried to console me. I told him that I thought I was losing my mind.

We got in the car, and he drove me those four blocks to my house. By the time he pulled into the driveway, my panic attack was in full force. Overwhelming feelings and fears of death hovered over my head, circling like vultures around a dead carcass. I started hyperventilating and sweating even more profusely. John ran into the house and told Debbie that they needed to take me to the hospital because I had freaked out. It had never been that severe before. I really thought I was going to die.

The trip to the hospital, only ten minutes away, seemed to last forever. The immense emotional pressure was overwhelming my mind and body. Prior to leaving, Debbie had called the troop and told them that I was having a panic attack. When we arrived at the emergency room, Sgt. Jerry Mayfield was there waiting for us. He tried to reassure me that I was going to be okay. At that point, I could not believe him. I thought that I was surely going to die.

Dr. Greer was also there waiting for me. He gave me a muscle relaxer and some Valium to try and calm me down. As I lay there on the gurney, my fears and anxiety finally subsided. After I had calmed down, Dr. Greer came back to my room. He took my hand and placed it in his.

"Bobby, I think we need to talk," he said. "I think you need some emotional help to deal with this trauma. You need help to deal with the grieving process of losing your career and sight." He then suggested that I see a psychologist to help me through this process.

I went home that evening and got a good night of rest, due only to the medication that Dr. Greer had given me.

When I got up the next morning, I began to think about what he had told me.

"Do I need a mental health professional?" I contemplated. "Am I losing my sanity? Am I crazy? I am a police officer. They pay me to handle tough and traumatic situations. I am supposed to always be in control. Is it possible that I am just human, and that I need to accept help, as well as give it? All of these thoughts ran through my head, causing more confusion. My greatest fear I had was that I would wind up in a mental institution totally blind, and be abused by the other patients. This compounded the fear of admitting that I needed help.

Days came and went. Few were good. I began to call the bad days my "blind days." Those were the days when I despised being blind. Those days, I literally hated my new world of darkness, and I hated the fact that I was now forced to live in it.

On one "blind day," I found myself curled up in a fetal position, in the corner of my bedroom, sobbing uncontrollably. I could not make myself stop, and the pain would not go away. I sincerely wanted to die. I hadn't actually contemplated suicide before this. I had never gone to my dresser and picked up my .357 magnum and stuck it to my head, wanting to blow my brains out. I had never grabbed a handful of pain pills and stuffed them in my mouth to make all the pain go away so I could die quietly. I had never taken any of those overt actions. I wanted the emotional pain to go away so desperately. I had been to policemen's funerals. I had heard of policemen who had committed suicide, and I didn't quite understand why anyone would take their own life. I thought it was a cowardly way to leave your friends, family and everything they had believed in. I used to not understand that, but it was all clear to me now. What seemed to be irrational thoughts to me then, were now totally rational. Death seemed to be the only way out of this emotionally traumatized life I now led. I needed help, and if I didn't get it, I was afraid of what might happen.

I picked up the phone and dialed the number that Dr. Greer had given me, to make an appointment to see the psychologist. The next day, when I arrived at the psychologist's office, I was unsure about what he would think of me. I wondered if he would think I was crazy and have me institutionalized, or would he put me on a number of medications and turn me into a zombie? I just wanted to be myself again so badly!

I was not impressed with my first session, to say the least. He would not let me tell my story. He wouldn't let me talk about the terrible emotional pain I was going through. He wouldn't let me talk about the shooting, the nightmares, or the flashbacks. He only wanted to give me drugs to help me deal with the anxiety. I wanted help, not drugs.

The second session was just like the first.

"When can I talk," I asked him. "When can I tell you what I am dealing with?"

He told me that we would talk when they got my blood leveled out. I told him I didn't think I could wait that long. He assured me that we would talk the next week.

The third week was the same as the first and second. I was smart enough to know that this was not going to work. If your mechanic doesn't fix your car correctly, you need to get another one. If your barber doesn't cut your hair right, you find a new one. It was time for me to find a new shrink.

CHAPTER 24
WHAT HAPPENED TO THE LIGHT?

It was mid morning, Debbie had gone to work, and I was feeling a little more comfortable about being at home alone. I was learning to cope with the remaining anxiety. There were times when I would look directly at a light, or look into the bright sunshine, coming through the window, and see some light. No objects or images, but I could tell if I was looking directly at a light.

I sat on the couch and began to watch TV. I turned on the lamp next to me, in case someone came by to see me. Also, I didn't want to be sitting there in the dark. This was also one of the few attempts I made to make myself look like a normal sighted person. As I turned the lamp on, I noticed that my light had disappeared. I thought maybe the bulb had burned out, or maybe the lamp had been unplugged. I reached down behind the end table feeling along the cord and discovered that the lamp had not been unplugged. I placed my hand near the bulb and could feel heat. I knew then that the light was on, but I couldn't tell. I turned the lamp off and placed my face directly in front of the light bulb. Then I turned it on and opened my eyes. Still, there was no light! I could feel panic overtake my body. Boy, could I feel the cold, dark fear.

"Was this it?" I asked myself. "Was my little ray of hope going to abandon me to this unforgiving world of total darkness?"

I stood and hurriedly walked across the room, down the hall, through the bedroom and into my bathroom. There was a row of Hollywood lights across my vanity that I thought would surely be bright enough for me to see. I looked up at the lights and turned them on. Dull, black nothing! Once again I placed my hand on a bulb to see if there was heat coming from the light and there was. But there was no light for me.

Hoping that I was mistaken, I closed my eyes and turned the light switch on once again. Still, nothing! A monumental feeling of hopelessness overcame my whole being. I turned the light switch off and walked into the bedroom. I sat down on the bed and began to cry.

I turned my eyes toward heaven and asked God, "Why, God, why did you take my little ray of light, my only little ray of hope, from me?" I sobbed and begged God, "Please, give me back my sight, please, God." At once I felt the presence of someone. I reached out, but no one was there. No one was physically there, but I felt the warmth and presence of someone there with me. This feeling was a familiar one, it reminded me of the one I had felt as a child, when I would stump my toe and run to my mom for her comfort. She would caress me to her breast, console me, and tell me that it was going to be okay. I had always felt safe in my mom's arms. That feeling had ended with her death, but now it had reoccurred. This feeling was very unusual.

Then I heard a voice. It was not an audible voice, but I felt it in my heart. The voice said to me, "Bobby, you don't need that light because I am the light, and I will show you the way." My mom had been right, God is always there for us if we will accept Him.

At that moment I began to pray, "God, please forgive me for all the things I have done. Please forgive me for failing to serve you God, I'm asking you to come into my heart and give me another chance to serve you. I'll be a better man, father, husband, and Christian if you'll just help me."

CHAPTER 25
BUT MIKE, I THINK I CAN DRIVE

It had been three months since I had last exercised. The doctor told me that it was now okay for me to work-out again. I called Mike Epps and Jackie Coleman to see what they were doing that morning. They were not busy, so I asked them if they would come get me and take me by the troop and work-out. Some people work-out to get rid of stress, but I was addicted to it. Prior to my shooting, I had been training for a regional meet in the southern portion of the United States. While I was out of commission, I had exercise withdrawal. I needed to get back in the gym.

In just a while, I heard a pick-up truck pull in the driveway. Surely, it was Mike and Jackie. I went to meet them at the door, and Mike was waiting there for me. I grabbed his arm and started toward the truck. Jackie was sitting in the passenger's side, and I assumed that Mike was taking me to the passenger's side, but I was wrong. Mike took me to the driver's side of the truck and told me to get in. Still assuming that I was on the passenger's side, I raised my left leg to step onto the floorboard.

As I tried to find the floorboard of the truck, I continued to raise my left leg and step into the truck. Empty air met my foot. Mike started yelling at me to get into the truck and stop playing around. I told him that I was not playing and was trying. He told me that I was embarrassing him, and people were staring at us. My foot finally connected with what I thought was the floorboard but was actually his door, and my foot slid right off. I was getting confused and agitated.

"Where was I?" Mike began laughing, still telling me to get in the truck.

I had already learned as an infant blind person that when I got confused, I needed to stop, regain my composure, figure out where I was and start over. I began feeling around and realized that I was on the driver's side.

"Mike, you've got me on the driver's side."

"I never said that you were anywhere else."

"I assumed I was on the passenger's side," I said. "Why didn't you tell me?"

"There you go, assuming again. You know what assuming does, and here lately, you've been making that saying come true a lot!"

I got into the truck and slid into the middle to sit between Mike and Jackie. Jackie was leaned on the door laughing at Mike.

"Man, why do you treat Bobby like that? You aren't right," Jackie complained.

"I'm not right, I'm sick and tired of this blind pity stuff," Mike quickly replied. "You act like there is something wrong with him. There's nothing wrong with him. This is a free ride for him, and he loves it!"

Mike and Jackie were two of my best friends. Jackie and I worked in the same parish as resident troopers together. Mike worked out of the troop, but all three of us had been friends for years. They were the ones I turned to when I would have breakdowns in the middle of the night. They were always there, just like most of the guys from the troop.

That day we were like three junior high boys: laughing, joking and poking fun at each other. We were just having fun, just like we always had before the shooting. We drove a couple of blocks and stopped at a little corner grocery store called Cox's Grocery. I had been there thousands of times.

When I was a state trooper, I would stop there for a soda and a snack. I could still visualize exactly how everything was laid out at the store. I could see the gas pumps, the front door and the small shopping center across the street.

Mike stopped his truck at the front door, jumped out and told us that he was going to get us a soda and would be right back. I don't know what came over me. I suddenly had this strong urge to drive. I looked at Jackie and asked him if there was anything behind us.

He turned and looked, then asked, "No, there's nothing, why do you ask?"

I told him that I was going to drive Mike's truck.

"You must be crazy," he replied.

I assured him that I would be able to do it if he would just let me know if there was anything coming.

I slid into the driver's seat and cranked the truck. Mike was an avid hunter, and like most hunters, Mike loved his truck. I asked Jackie if there was anything coming and he said "no" so I put the truck in reverse and started backing up. This was great; I was driving! I stopped the truck and put it in drive. Again, I asked Jackie if it was clear for me to go, and he assured me that it was okay.

I had gone maybe twenty or thirty feet when Jackie yelled for me to stop because there was a car pulling in the parking lot. I slammed on the brakes. I was getting ready to start again when I heard a familiar scream. It was Mike coming out of the store. He sounded like a panther screaming as he ran across the parking lot. He was hollering and yelling at me.

"Are you crazy?" he hollered. "You must have brain damage from that shooting! I can't believe you're driving my truck!"

Before I could move, Mike pushed me over and got

in the driver's seat, still screaming and yelling at me. Jackie and I were both laughing hysterically because we thought all of this was extremely funny. I don't think Mike saw the same humor we did. He threw our drinks in our laps.

Mike looked at Jackie and said, "I thought there was at least one responsible person in this truck, but now I know that I am the only responsible person here."

Jackie and I continued to laugh.

Mike turned to me and asked, "Do you think this is funny?"

"I think it is extremely funny. Why are you getting so upset about a pick-up truck?"

"I love this truck. It is my pride and joy! I can't believe you drove my truck!"

Jackie and I continued to laugh, all the way to the troop. Mike was still furious, "Oh, you think that's funny," he ranted. I still thought it was funny even though Mike jabbed me, squarely in my ribs, every time he asked me that question.

We finally got to the troop and parked in the back with the other police units. When Mike stopped the truck, he immediately grabbed me by the arm and started pulling me out of the truck. We were still laughing, but mostly at how mad Mike had gotten.

As Mike began pulling me out of the truck, my knees hit the driver's door and a sharp pain ran up my legs. "You still think it's funny," Mike asked. I agreed that it was still funny, even with the pain that was seizing my legs.

Mike got me out of the truck and started walking really fast toward the troop. This was not a good thing for me, because when you are blind, you must move slower than sighted people in case you run into something. It gives you more reaction time. I knew that I would have no reaction time at the rate of speed Mike was pulling me. Small steps up or down can cause a blind person to tumble to the ground easily. I asked him to slow down, but he replied, "No, you think it's funny."

About that time, Mike rounded the front of one of the units sitting in the parking lot — way too close on my side. There it was again, that excruciating pain in my legs, because Mike had cut the corner too close and ran me into the push bumper on the front of that unit. I hollered at him in pain. He looked at me and once again asked, "You still think it's funny?" Being somewhat hard headed I still agreed that I thought it was funny. Boy, was that a mistake.

He continued to drag me across the parking lot and I knew that the side walk to the back entrance should be coming up soon but I wasn't sure when. I was right. I felt him step up, but he was moving so quickly that I could not react to his step in time and my toe hit the step. I began stumbling, almost falling, and Mike yanked me up, still moving at his fast pace. Once again he asked, "You still think it's funny?" Unknowing what snares were still lying ahead, I once again agreed that it was still funny.

I had become very alert, trying to anticipate what was going to come next. I knew that we would be coming to the double doors at the back entrance soon, but I was still trying to regain my balance from the step.

Mike screamed, "Come on, if you think it's so funny." Mike quickly approached the double doors and opened the left door and started through. I assumed that the right door was also open; it was not. I ran face first into that metal door. Once again Mike asked, "You still think it's funny?"

Enough was enough, "No, I don't think it's nearly as funny as I did a while ago," I replied.

Jackie told Mike that he shouldn't have been treating

me like that, because he was going to hurt me.

Mike quickly replied, "You can't hurt him. He has already proven that. He got shot in the head with a shotgun and that didn't hurt him. Why do you think running him into a door is going to hurt him?"

Some of the troopers were in the back parking lot and saw Mike running me into things. They yelled at him to stop.

Mike yelled back, "When are you going to learn to stop treating him like an invalid or something? This is the way I treated him when he could see. Why should I change the way I treat him now?"

Mike was right. He was probably the only one that had treated me like he always had We had gone hunting together, worked out, and worked the roads. We had a lot of fun together. Mike didn't want to lose that. He wanted things to be the way they were. Oh, how we all wanted things to be the way they were.

We went in the gym and got a quick, fun work-out. It was great to pump the iron once again and it made me feel good. We left the weight room and went to the front of the troop and visited with some of the troopers before we left.

As we walked out, Mike told me, "Bobby, there is your unit, do you want to go by and see it?" I agreed, and we walked over to the car. I still had my keys, so I unlocked the door and sat down in the driver's seat. I adjusted the steering wheel, just as I had always done before and cranked my unit. A crushing feeling of sadness came over me, and tears began to roll down my face. As I sat there, I recalled the last time I had sat in that seat, 11:30 p.m., March 14th. At that moment, our little adventure had ceased being fun.

PHOTO
ALBUM

Bobby is with his partner,
Jackie Coleman

*Sammy Rogers, Bobby's close friend
and workout partner*

The violator's vehicle,
following the shooting

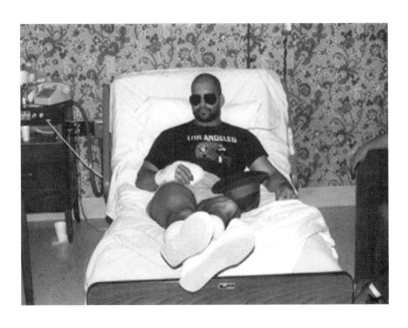

Bobby in St. Francis Hospital,
one week following the shooting

Bobby is being escorted to the plane that will take him to Memphis.

Ron Scammerhorn of the Tennessee
State Police, who was our escort
during our stay at Memphis

Kim Smith a year after the shooting

*Bobby is receiving his purple
heart from Dr. Spencer Campbell*

Janie aboard Marine 1 helicopter

Kim Smith at age 15, holding brother
Brad Elliot Smith, during 1990

Kim at age 16,
Brad at age 1

Brad Elliot Smith
age 5

Kim Smith at age 22,
Brad Smith at age 7

*Bobby, escorted by Kim, receives his
diploma from Dr. Dwight D. Vines*

Bobby, Janie and Kim, as Maid of Honor at West Monroe High School Homecoming

Bobby and Janie were featured on the
Louisiana State Trooper Association Magazine
when he met President Ronald Reagan.

Brad,
high school football picture

Jason Smith
Louisiana State Trooper
Bobby's nephew

Bobby's presentation at the
Time Warner Stockholder's Annual Conference lead to
the removal of the album "Cop Killer"

Brad, Janie and Bobby

Danny McNight family photo,
Forte Fundraiser, 2005

CHAPTER 26
"I'LL TAKE F-18"
Trooper Mike Epps
Louisiana State Police

Following Bobby's return from Memphis after his eye surgery, Jackie and I spent at least half of our shift with Bobby at his house. Those were the days that seemed to be the toughest, because of the problems Bobby was having, in addition to the state police trying to screw him over.

One day, while I was at Bobby's house, he asked me to go into his room and make sure his uniform still looked good, his brass was shined, and everything was in the right place. This was also when Bobby's anxiety attacks started, especially at night. For some reason, at about 10 p.m. every night Bobby would have the worst episodes. He would call Jackie and I to come over to his house and be with him.

I went to Bobby's house at night when he called to try and comfort him. The only thing I could think of to do was to try and make him forget about what was upsetting him. The only way I knew to do that, was to treat him the way I had always treated him. I cracked jokes – anything to lighten the mood when I got there. I desperately wanted things to get back to normal.

The first thing I did each night when I got to his house was check his food supply. If I thought the food supply was low, I would let him know. I told him that if he was going to call us over all of the time, he was going to have to keep some food, especially yogurt raisins, in the cabinets. I felt that the best way to get him through this time was with humor. Laughter seemed to take his mind off the trauma.

Sometimes I brought him to my house so that he could be with someone, and also because I knew that we always had groceries (just kidding). Mindy, my daughter, was five and Ryan, my son, was about two then. The most prominent memory I have is of Bobby lying on the couch, and Ryan trying to show Bobby his throwing ability. After that, I couldn't help but laugh because when Bobby heard those little feet running through the house, he would grab his head and curl up to protect himself. Ryan never understood why Bobby would never try to catch the ball. Although, he sure did get a big laugh when he bounced the ball off of Bobby's head.

The new surroundings didn't seem to help. Every night around 10 p.m., no matter where Bobby was, he would get depressed and start crying. The times he spent at our house were always special ones. My family grew to love him during this time we spent together.

To this day, I feel that Mindy and Ryan are more understanding of people with physical disabilities because of the time we spent with Bobby. Because of him, they see people as individuals, and not necessarily disabled people.

Annette is one of the greatest wives in the world, and this became even more obvious during that time. Being a State Trooper took so much time, and then, when I was off duty, I would try to spend time with Bobby also. Annette was so understanding during that time.

I remember Bobby telling me that he was a cowboy, when cowboys weren't cool. Well, Bobby, Jackie and myself spent time walking around in public, arm in arm, before that kind of thing was cool. I guess we could do that now and everyone would just think that we were Clinton supporters, but back then, we really got some weird looks. Some of my favorite times with Bobby were when I would mess with him and run him into things. I will never forget that time when Bobby decided to drive my truck. I will never forget that feeling that came over me when I stepped out of that store and saw my truck moving. Then when I realized it was Bobby driving, not Jackie, I went crazy!

Then, there was the curse of F-18. When the commander of the troop decided that he would reissue Bobby's license plate F-18 to someone else, Jackie and I were furious. I tried to get Jackie to take the plate and put it on his unit, but he never would. I'm glad he never did though, because as tender hearted as Jackie is, he would have had to stop his unit and cry every time he called F-18 to Troop F.

Well, I finally decided to take my plate F-48 off and replace it with Bobby's plate F-18. That was a big mistake on my part. A few months later, I started suffering headaches. Not just your everyday, take a couple of Advil headaches. I'm talking, throw-your-guts-up, back-the-car-over-my-head and take-me-out-of-my-misery type headaches. I went to the emergency room one night and woke up the next morning feeling like I had been run over by a car. When I opened my eyes I thought I must have died and gone to hell, because the first thing I saw was Bobby, Jackie and Charlie Heard standing at the foot of my bed. Then I did what anyone would have done if they woke up to a sight like that, I rolled over and puked.

When I rolled back over, I was expecting at least a little sympathy from my friends, but all I heard was Jackie telling Bobby and Charlie how amazed he was that someone could vomit so quietly. He was astounded. Jackie then started describing vividly how he throws up, and that was all I needed. I began again. Then I heard Jackie telling Bobby that his shooting and my cerebral meningitis were caused by the curse of F-18.

Some time thereafter, I left the state police and went to work for Customs. That was when Jackie gave up his plate, F-46, and took Bobby's plate, F-18, and put it on his unit. We were doing whatever we could to keep anyone else from getting Bobby's plate. Three years passed, and the curse struck once again. Jackie was diagnosed with cancer but has been in remission for several years. That was when we thought it would be best to take F-18 somewhere and drive a wooden stake in it. While Jackie had Bobby's plate, there was a request made, and the plate was retired.

When I was hired with U.S. Customs, I remember telling Bobby about my new job, and he said that we should have a party because they would never see me again. We had that party at Jackie's, and it was tough because I really believed Bobby when he said that we would probably never see each other again. We had been through so much together during the last few years and the three of us had become very close. When I walked out of Jackie's house that night, I really believed that we would never be together again. When I went out of service that last time and shook Jackie's hand, it was very emotional for me because I knew I would miss our friendship and didn't know who was going to take care of Jackie now. I was walking away, not only from a part of my life that was the most precious I had experienced, but away from a friendship with two people that most people never get to experience but once in their lifetime, if at all.

God sure works in mysterious ways, because look at us now. I moved back to West Monroe and as a Customs agent, I get to follow up on Criminal Patrol investigations. After all we had been through, and now we are all back together again.

I could go on forever about the times we had — both

fun and not so fun. I will never forget the last time my dad was in the hospital. He was doing really bad and was asleep or unconscious most of the time, but one night he came to while I was standing next to his bed looking down at him. He looked up at me, smiled and we began talking about what I had done that day. I told him that I had been with Bobby, and he asked how Bobby was doing. I told him that he was doing pretty good. My dad looked up at me and said, "Mike, don't you walk away from Bobby because a lot of people that are around him now will. He will need real friends like you for the hard times that lie ahead of him."

I hoped that when Bobby looked back on our friendship that he didn't see me as a friend just because I was a fellow trooper. I wanted him to see me as the kind of friend my daddy had taught me to be. I loved Bobby as a brother.

VISIONS OF COURAGE

166

CHAPTER 27
IT'S HARD TO FIX A
BROKEN GLASS

It was becoming clear to me about what psychologists say about major losses in our lives, and how those losses create tremendous amounts of stress. The loss of your job or career, problems with health or disability, the loss or decrease in your wages, all create financial burdens, problems in your marriage and/or divorce. I was already experiencing the first three, and the latter seemed inevitable.

Debbie and I had been married for five years. There were a lot of good times, but there were lots of things that were missing. One was the lack of serious commitment to one another and to our marriage. The fact that I spent half of my time as a State Trooper didn't help. The parish I had been assigned to was 85 miles from our home in Monroe. I had to have a separate residence there to utilize while I was working. Besides the distance in miles, there was a distance in our relationship that had been created by this physical separation. We knew we had problems before the shooting, and now the shooting had created even worse problems. My being shot had been tremendously hard for her. She was used to the independent, self-sufficient person that I was before the shooting, and now all of that was gone.

Debbie had worked hard in establishing her career, and now she was being forced to be a caretaker for her disabled, blind husband. It was emotionally and physically strenuous. Many times we sat on the couch together, trying to figure out what we were going to do. We were trying so hard to put our marriage back together, and it was extremely difficult. We were both emotionally bankrupt from trying to deal with the trauma and adjusting to this life, in order to fit into this new world we had been cast into. Saving this marriage was more than either of us could handle. We decided a separation was probably best for both of us. We needed some relief.

She moved into an apartment just down the street from our house, and I stayed in the house. I had never felt so alone and destitute in my entire life. That old familiar dragon of panic returned.

CHAPTER 28
THE DRAGON

I didn't like being by myself, so I made sure that there was always someone there with me during the day. Sometimes in the evenings I would go to some of the officer's homes and spend time with them. But, eventually I would have to return, alone, to my house. I hated being there by myself in the darkness. It wasn't just my physical darkness that plagued me. It was also the nighttime. There was something bad about the nighttime. The bad things always seemed to happen then, and I didn't understand why.

The dragon seemed to be there at night. Sometimes he brought his friends: fear, anxiety, paranoia, insecurity, insomnia and, in addition, I had to fight with the uncontrollable sobbing. I couldn't sleep much at night, if any at all. I was afraid of what was out there that I couldn't see. My not being able to see on March 14th was what had got me into all of this mess. Would I be harmed again?

I would lay in my bed with all the lights out so that if anyone looked in my window, they couldn't see me. I would lie there in silence listening. Was someone lurking out there in the shadows? Did I actually hear that noise I thought I heard? I thought I heard someone walking in the back yard. Was it my imagination or was it real?

The mind can play horrible tricks on you especially after a severe trauma. One of my greatest fears was the potential of someone harming me again. You can't defend yourself when you can't see when it is coming, or where it is coming from. This paranoia would bring about auditory hallucinations (hearing sounds that weren't there). My mind was so powerful. It seemed like every time I laid down, I would begin to hear all kinds of sounds. The most common I heard was the sound of someone walking down the hall, into my bedroom and standing right over me. I could actually hear them breathing, right over me. I wondered, "What should I do? Should I try to get to the phone? Should I just lay as still as I could and maybe they wouldn't know I was there. I would literally lay there paralyzed by fear, with feelings of suffocation. There were times I wanted to move but couldn't because it was so terrifying.

I'm not sure why, but the worst panic attacks usually happened around 3 a.m. That was when I would call Mike or Jackie. Sometimes when Mike answered the phone I couldn't respond to him because all I could do was cry. He knew it was me and would ask me if I was OK.

I would finally get a "no," out in the midst of all the wailing. He assured me that he was on his way, and that he would be there in just a few minutes. When I hung up with Mike, I called Jackie. I knew Mike lived further away so I wanted him to be en route the quickest. Then I would call Jackie and get him on his way. Then I called the troop and talked with the desk sergeant until they arrived. They always came, poor ole Mike and Jackie. They never got any sleep back then because of me, but they always came.

By the time they got to the house, I had already begun to feel somewhat better because I knew I could count on them. They were my own personal cavalry, who never failed to come to my rescue. They would come in, we would cry, laugh, and then we would cry some more. None of us knew what we should have done, but just being together made all the difference in the world. The event usually ended the same, with me packing some bags and going to spend a few days with Mike. By this time, Mike's wife and children were used to the routine.

CHAPTER 29
THE BLIND SCHOOL

I went back to counseling to deal with some of the issues I had. The loss of my sight, the loss of my career, and the loss of my marriage. My psychologist advised me that it was time to accept the fact that I was blind and most likely would be for the rest of my life, and that I needed to prepare myself as a blind person. He said I needed to go to blind school to get some special training.

The blind school was located in Ruston, just 30 miles west of Monroe. Also located in Ruston was Louisiana Tech University, nationally known for their women's basketball team, the Lady Techsters, who had won numerous national championships. There were also other great athletes that had come from Tech. Terry Bradshaw was one who went on to play for the Pittsburgh Steelers and had become one of the greatest quarterbacks ever. The "Mailman," Karl Malone, who had left Tech and went to play professional basketball for the Utah Jazz, was another. Ruston was also famous for its peaches, and it was the home of the Louisiana Peach Festival.

Neither Ruston nor Tech was one of my favorite places. During my college years, I attended Northeast Louisiana University, which was one of the biggest rival schools of Tech. To say that we didn't really care for each other was putting the rivalry mildly. We were the Northeast Indians, and they were the Louisiana Tech Bulldogs. It didn't really matter who won or lost, but the competition was always exciting. I had to go to enemy territory, and on top of that, I was going to blind school. I absolutely did not want to be there!

The ride to Ruston seemed to last forever. The dragon was there with his pals once again - fear, anxiety, and paranoia. What if I get run over by a truck while trying to cross the road? What if someone mugs me, or even worse, what if someone kills me? Aren't blind people easy prey? I was 5'11", 185 pounds, a competitive power lifter, a macho state trooper, physically fit to the bone, but why was I so afraid?

When we pulled into the parking lot of the blind school, my hands were shaking and my palms were wet. I could feel the effects of the anxiety in my body. I just wanted to run away, and I knew I couldn't do that without hurting myself.

There were five steps leading to the front door, and I stumbled on every one. Man, I thought, what a pitiful blind person I was. But one thing was for sure, none of the students were staring out of the window, watching me blunder up the steps. My mom, dad, Terry, and Betty were waiting in the foyer when I finally entered the front door to my new adventure. They were talking to Ms. Hernandez, the blind director of the blind school.

Ms. Hernandez stuck out her hand to shake mine, but how was I supposed to know that? She told me, "Here's my hand, shake my hand."

"I would if I knew where it was," I replied. Wasn't this going to be a sight, two blind people trying to find each other's hands? It wasn't worth the effort to me. Why wasn't a simple "hello" good enough?

I already had a bad attitude about blind school, and I hadn't even started. Ms. Hernandez walked us through the school introducing us to some of the other blind people there. Once again, there was that same old hand shaking routine. Man, I've got to get better at this, I thought. As she walked us through the school, she would tell me what every room was when she got to it, trying to familiarize me with my new surroundings. When she had brought us to the computer room, she told me that this would be where I would take my computer classes. Computers, you mean blind people can type on computers? I could barely operate one when I could see, much less now that I am totally blind.

Next we came to the reading room. This is where you will learn to read and write Braille. I sat down in a chair, and she handed me a book. She said, "Run your finger over that." I did. It was just a bunch of dots and it meant nothing to me. I wondered, how could anybody read that garbage because it all seemed to run together?

"This is the kitchen; we are going to teach you how to cook," she explained. Wow, this is going to be great! A blind guy in the kitchen with a bunch of sharp knives and an open flame! My attitude got worse with every step.

She then introduced me to the staff. Louis was my favorite; he was the one who was going to teach me cane travel. He was a track star from California who had lost his eyesight after college.

We left the school and went to the living quarters. It was about a quarter of a mile away. I was driven this time, but after that, I would be on my own to navigate this unfamiliar course. I learned that route very well because I had to walk back and forth at least twice a day, sometimes three times. The route went down the street and over a bridge with no side rails. I wondered how many blind students they had lost crossing this bridge. We took a right and went about 200 more yards and then left into the blind school apartment parking lot.

At that time, I was handed a white cane and told that tomorrow I would walk to school with the rest of the stu-

173

dents. I thought that they had to be joking. Like this stick was going to help me find my way back to that school a quarter of a mile away. This has got to be a sick joke! This was going to be worse than dealing with Mike Epps!

As a Trooper, I was sometimes assigned to Lincoln Parish, which is the parish where the blind school was located. Many times before, I had parked on the side of the streets in Ruston and watched those blind students tap down the sidewalk. Never in a million years did I ever think that one day I would be among them. I had been indifferent about those blind people tapping down the street, stopping at the street corner, who didn't look both ways but listened both ways. I didn't realize that was what they were doing then. I used to wonder how they kept from getting run over. I noticed the manhole covers on the sidewalks as I watched them tap down the sidewalk. I wondered if someone left a manhole open, and the students couldn't see it, if they would just step right in the middle of it and get washed away in the river or something. Wow, I thought it must be scary being blind.

I wondered who matched the clothes for those people. How did they figure out which shirt to wear with which pants? Maybe some of them just didn't care.

Ms. Hernandez opened the door to my apartment and we walked in it.

She said, "To the left is your kitchen, straight ahead is the living room and this way to your bedroom."

"This way," I said, " which way is this way?" To the right is your bedroom she had told me. Yea, but where is that coffee table, I wondered.

We unloaded my belongings from the car, and I settled in. I made the bed, put my groceries away and then we sat around and visited for a while. Then everyone left. I was there alone. "Not again," I begged my subconscious.

"Please, don't wake the dragons!"

I found my way back through the living room, past the coffee table and into the bedroom. I laid down on the bed and cried in hopes of crying myself to sleep. I had done that too many times before, but at least it would give me some sleep. I curled up in the fetal position on my bed. I was afraid like a little child. The little boy was afraid, and he wanted his mama!

I was already up, dressed and had my breakfast when I heard a knock at my door the next morning.

"Bobby, I'm Ms. Riddle. I am one of the instructors at the school and I'm going to help you to school this morning," she said.

I started walking out the door, and she reminded me not to forget my cane. I had already forgotten about that, I was used to a sighted guide. I had been blind for five months, and was accustomed to grabbing someone's arm and them helping me anywhere I needed to go.

"Step up, Bobby, now step down, and now we are going to go up three steps," she instructed. "Stop, and now turn right," she continued. I was accustomed to having these types of instructions, but this was about to come to an end. Insecure about this whole thing, I reached out and grabbed her arm. She stopped, "I'll let you use my arm this time, but from now on, you will use your cane," she informed me. I had seen those blind people before tapping with that stick, but I didn't know what that meant. I didn't understand how they could do that without running into something, and now I was being told that I too would have to use that cane as my way of transportation. Man, this is worse than going back to the first grade, I thought.

We arrived at the school. My first day at blind school; what a treat. You guessed it; my attitude wasn't any better than it was the day before. I didn't want to be there, I didn't want to be blind, and I didn't want to associate with a bunch of blind people running into each other and running into walls. None of this seemed very exciting or fun to me. I was used to having fun. I used to have a job that was exciting. I loved putting the drunks, rapists, and murderers in jail. That was fun and exciting; this was not.

When we finally got there, everyone was standing in the foyer of the school. Then I heard Ms. Hernandez ask if everyone was there. I wondered how she would know if anyone was missing, no one there could see. She went on to introduce me to the other students. I was the new student, oh yea. She went on to tell them that I was a police officer and had gotten shot in the face several months ago and was blind.

"Let's welcome Bobby to our school," she said. A round of applause broke out. Yeah, yeah, yeah big deal.

I could hear someone tapping over to me. It was Louis.

"Bobby, this is Louis, put it there," he said.

I thought, "Oh God, here we go again with that hand shake thing." I started to think that maybe it would be a good idea if we would all put bells on our hands. Then we could locate each other's hands since they seemed to want to shake hands so much. Louis was a good guy with a great, outgoing personality. He was tall and thin, ideal for a distance runner. We hit it off pretty well.

"Bobby, follow me," he said. "We are going to the classroom, and I am going to give ya'll some assignments on cane travel."

"Cane travel, you mean I'm going to have to go outside and walk by myself," I wondered aloud.

"Well not just yet. I'm going to have to teach you

how first. I'm going with you."

I remember sarcastically contemplating how Louis was also blind. I thought that was just great. A blind person is going to go walking with me. This is going to be terrific. It really would be like the old saying about the "blind leading the blind."

"Hold your hand right about your navel and extend your cane to the ground. Rotate your wrist from the left to the right. Tap to the left, and tap to the right," he instructed. It seemed simple enough and that it would work to keep me out of danger, but I was still concerned about how this "wonderful" cane could protect me from open manhole covers.

We then left the classroom, walked out the door and across the front porch. Louis was in front of me, and he told me that we were coming up to the steps. He said that I should put my cane out in front of me so I could feel the step and continue until I got down to the ground.

"How do you know how many steps there are?" I asked.

"Well, just keep putting your cane down until it won't go down anymore."

"How do I know if I am too far to the left or right? What if I fall off?"

"Well, you just have to be careful."

Boy, was that encouraging, I thought, as my sarcastic attitude grew.

We walked across the parking lot. I could hear traffic coming. I could also feel the breeze blowing and felt the sun shining on my face. As a blind person, all of these factors would become very important to me in cane travel. I would learn to listen to the traffic to determine the direction of the traffic. Being able to feel the wind and sun on my face was to become very important to me because it would help me determine my direction. I also utilized the fact that the sun always rises in the East and sets in the West. Gravely, I realized that those small things I used to take for granted now carried a great significance in my life.

We tapped through the parking lot, around the cars, and finally to the edge of the street. We stopped, listened and crossed the street. We actually made it to the other side safely. We walked down the sidewalk for a couple of blocks and then crossed another street, and then another, and another and then we turned around and came back the same way. Maybe this isn't going to be so bad, I thought. I didn't hurt myself. As a matter of fact, I can see this as an adventure. I had safely ventured out into my new, unforgiving wilderness, with my eyes closed, with my stick in my hand, trying to find my way around.

For a week, Louis and I cane traveled everyday for an hour. He was teaching me how to cross the street safely; how to know when the traffic was stopped and all the other important details.

I was ready for my maiden voyage; I was ready to go out on my own. Louis gave me a route to take, a place to go to, an item to purchase, and a receipt to show proof that I had made it there successfully. I was ready for the challenge. I was feeling good about myself. I had been in blind school for a week. My attitude hadn't changed very much about being there, but this was something different. I would get to go out on my own, to see if I could brave the highway, sidewalks and construction sites and get to a destination and then return safely.

I started tapping down the sidewalk, proud of myself. I was on my way home. I made it to my location, bought the item, got the receipt and started back. Tapping down the sidewalk very confidently, I encountered something I had never thought about before. It was what most blind people wished never to hear, a charging, barking dog.

My dad had always said that as long as a dog is barking, he can't bite. But, when you hear a dog running toward you barking, and you don't know if he is behind a fence or not, that fight or flight syndrome will kick in. My initial thought was to run. I took about half a step and realized, "What are you doing? You are blind! You can't just take off running! What if you run into the street and get run over? What if you hit a telephone pole? Was that manhole covered?" Then I realized, my best bet was to stay and fight.

I wheeled around to face the charging dog, and he was still barking. He was getting closer and closer, and I was getting more terrified, but I didn't know what else to do. I stood there as still as I could, staring at the dog, as he charged toward me. At that time I figured, if you can't beat them, you might as well join them. I crouched down and started barking back at the dog as sternly and as intimidating as I could. It worked! The dog stopped barking! Oh no, the silence was worse than the barking! I realized that the noise was the most important thing! I couldn't see him so I had to listen to figure out the location of the dog. I couldn't hear anything. I wondered where he was and what was his next move. I remembered again about what my dad had told me about a barking dog.

I swung my cane around like a Kung Fu fighter. Bruce Lee would have been proud! I jumped and kicked and screamed like a banshee and my cane became my Samurai sword. The dog still made no sound. Well, I guessed that I scared him.

I regained my composure and starting tapping down the sidewalk still terrified inside. Then, I started to laugh at myself. I wondered how many people were watching me thinking that crazy blind guy must have lost his mind. I began to laugh out loud. I must have looked like Don Quixote trying to fight the windmill. Well, I finally made it back to school from my great adventure.

I enjoyed cane travel because Louis was a warm, caring person. He cared about us and truly wanted to help blind people function in this world.

There was one other teacher that I really enjoyed. Her name was Gwen Page, she was the home economics teacher. She was a sighted woman. Her husband was a blind Baptist preacher, so she knew what it took for a blind person to function in this sighted world. They said she was black, but that didn't matter to me. In my world, everyone was black. You could tell by her voice that she smiled often. I guess it is true that when you lose one of your senses, the others are that much more enhanced. I was beginning to be able to tell things about people without seeing them.

Gwen taught us to feel a knife carefully to determine which side was the cutting edge. She also taught us how to cook, how to feel for heat, and how to use measuring cups. These were things that I had always taken for granted. It was amazing how much I learned from Gwen.

Gwen was a natural teacher, and she made learning fun. I didn't like the place, but when I was having fun, it was okay. Gwen and I really hit it off, and I loved being in her class. No doubt, I was her pet student. I was upset when she told me that her husband was probably going to get transferred in October, and she would have to quit working at the blind school.

I felt sorry for myself and for all blind people after I got shot. I never thought I would dislike any blind person. I was wrong. Sometimes there are people that you just don't like, and sometimes there is a good reason for it: they're just not nice people. There are some blind people that aren't nice, just as there are some sighted people that aren't. I learned more about life while I was in blind school than what was taught in the classes.

One blind student acted like a know-it-all and seemed very jealous of me. He would make slight insults and talk to me in a condescending manner. Needless to say, we argued often. I didn't care for him, and he didn't care for me. One day I was talking to a group of other students, and he started insulting me about being a state trooper. That was a huge mistake on his part, because being a state trooper had meant the world to me. As far as I was concerned, I still was a state trooper. I became angry and told him that if he didn't like what I was saying, he could always leave. He told me that if I didn't want him in the room, that I should make him leave as he threw back his chair.

Little did he know that I was a powder keg with a very short fuse. I had so much unprocessed anger and hostility bottled up inside of me, that all I needed was just the slightest spark to explode. He provided more than an adequate spark. I pushed my chair away and lunged across the table with one thought in mind: choking him down.

It didn't take a sighted person to realize that this was not the place to be. An auditory chaos began as students vacated their positions and frantically grabbed their canes to avoid the possibility of falling victim to my "blind" rage. That was the first time I ever heard what it sounds like when a blind person runs: a rapid tap, tap, tap, tap, tap, tap. There was so much of that going on all at once, that I realized I didn't have a clue as to where the loud-mouthed varmint went. Then, I began to come to my senses. What if I had grabbed the wrong fellow? What good would that have accomplished? "Loud mouth" would have really gotten some good material about police brutality then. I realized that everyone else must have feared that too, because they had all spilt, like scolded dogs. I saw the humor in this situation and couldn't help but to laugh out loud. I thought they were probably thinking that I had really gone out of my gourd, but I kept laughing anyway. I decided to let them believe that. I guess I had acted a little childishly, but I had had enough. That guy avoided me in the future, and I never heard another insult from him again or anyone else for that matter.

Things got somewhat tense at school one day. I was informed by a staff member that I couldn't go for a one day doctor's visit in Memphis because I didn't request formal approval beforehand. By this time, I was getting somewhat aggravated with all of their petty rules. I felt that all the students were being treated like kindergarteners instead of sensible adults. It seemed like some of the staff members wanted to run our lives and make us dependent on them. Needless to say, I went to Memphis.

I turned into somewhat of a rebel because of the way I felt about some of the staff members. Most of the students saw me as a leader, someone who would speak out to the staff on their behalf. The other students wouldn't talk back to the staff even if the staff member was wrong. There were probably times that I got a little carried away. I was even called a "radical" by one of the staff members. We were adults, not children, and I was not going to let them tell us what to do without voicing my opinion.

After some time, the students began speaking out. Obviously, the staff didn't like this, because they felt their authority was being questioned. The other blind students and I bonded with each other. We became unified and drew energy from one another. We were still individuals, but we were all members of a team.

Most of the students didn't have many visitors, and almost none of them had visitors during the week. My situation was much different. Just about every day I had a visitor. My younger brother, Kevin, was a student at Tech. He stopped by often and took me shopping.

I realized how important a car and driver were to a blind person. The other students would get really excited when my visitors came by, because there would always be an adventure. We would pack as many people as we could in Kevin's car, and then off we'd go. Kevin and I loved to take everyone shopping because it gave them a chance to get out, and they really loved it.

Lieutenant B.B. Lewis of the State Police lived in Ruston, and he stopped to visit me all of the time. He visited more than anyone while I was there. Sometimes we would just talk, and sometimes we would just ride around in his unit. He knew that I had a real fondness of frozen yogurt, so we'd stop by the yogurt shop during most of our outings. Once in a while he would bring my favorite yogurt with him: chocolate with crushed nuts on the top.

Other state troopers, police officers and deputies continued to visit with me. All these different officers were my bridge between the blind world and the sighted world. I figured the more time that I spent with them, and rode in their units, maybe I could still consider myself one of them. When I was with blind people, it made me feel like one of them, and I wasn't ready to accept that just yet.

One day we were all sitting in study period, and I heard a young lady's voice. Her voice was different; it was very slow and definitely not from any part of Louisiana. Some of the other students and I had been discussing birthdays.

I heard this voice ask me, "When is your birthday,

Bobby?"

I replied, "December 12th." She said that that was her birthday also, and then I heard someone leave the room.

I was intrigued by this lady, so I decided to ask her for her name. That was when I found out that when you are in a roomful of blind people, you must specify to whom you are talking to first. Otherwise, everyone answers when you ask a question.

One of the other ladies in the room finally asked me who I was talking to. I told her I was talking to the lady who had just asked me about my birthday. They told me her name was Jonell Standefer.

There was something special about her voice. It was so sweet, caring and compassionate. I soon found out more about Jonell. She was from New Mexico, and she had been blind for about a year. She had diabetic retinopathy, which caused her to slowly lose her sight, and now she was completely blind.

One day during class, I heard that same sweet voice again, asking the teacher a question. I knew it was Jonell. After class, I made my way over to where she was seated, introduced myself, and asked her if I could talk with her. In that same sweet voice, she assured me that she would be glad to talk with me. Since my marriage to Debbie was over, I needed a bond with someone. I wanted to share my thoughts with someone I could relate to and who would truly understand what I was going through. I needed to know someone who could accept me for who I am and what I was, a blind man.

Over a period of time, we got to know each other better. We shared our thoughts, deep feelings, dreams, and even our fears. Our friendship was strong, and each day we got closer. It seemed that the more we found out about each other, the more we had in common. We were both raised in the country, rodeoed in college, and born on December 12th. It was remarkable!

I needed to reach out to someone. Jonell was that someone. She taught me how to accept my blindness and how to be blind. Even though she was seven years younger than me, she taught me about life.

We did a lot of things together. We cooked and spent most of our time together. We were an item in blind school. We fell in love. I didn't know if our love was out of need, or if it was because we both wanted someone to care for us.

I still had some bad days, but they didn't seem to come as often. The nightmares and anxiety also seemed to subside. I was finally able to sleep, knowing that someone would be there waiting for me the next day, someone that I thought understood me and really cared for me: Jonell. I became very dependent on her and leaned heavily on her for emotional support, and she was always there. For the first time, I was beginning to do some things that I did when I was sighted. Her compassion helped me to feel happiness again. Once again, I began to laugh from the heart.

My rebellious heart gave me an idea one day. I shared it with Jonell, and she thought it was a good idea. I called Kevin and told him I needed him to take me to Wal-Mart that night. He agreed to do so, as usual, and came that evening as soon as class was out. When he got there, I told him we needed some spray paint, so we set out. Jonell stayed at the apartment and cooked supper for us while we were gone.

When we got there, I told Kevin that I needed a can of blue spray paint, and Jonell needed a can of hot pink spray paint. We got the paint and a few other things I needed and went to the check out. The lady rang my stuff up, leaned over the counter towards me and very slowly with a louder

185

than normal voice said, "That'll be twenty-three dollars and seventeen cents." I just stood there and smiled. I thought her misconception was humorous. She seemed to think that just because I was blind, I must have been hard of hearing or a little slow. She then started even slower and much louder telling me how much I owed. Kevin said, "He's blind, lady: he's not deaf!" The lady was so embarrassed and began apologizing profusely. I told her not to worry about it.

When we got back into the car, Kevin asked me what I was going to do with that spray paint. He was very curious as to why in the world two blind people wanted spray paint. I told him I would need his help, and as always, he agreed. I told him that Jonell and I would explain everything to him when we got back.

After dinner, Jonell and I explained that we wanted to be individuals and show our identity in our own way. I told him that we didn't want white canes like everyone else. I wanted a royal blue cane, the color of the state police, and Jonell wanted her cane hot pink. After we explained, Kevin took the paint and put coat after coat on the canes until the cans were empty. He said they looked great.

The next morning Jonell and I walked to school with our freshly painted canes. We walked with a few other students, but they didn't say anything about our canes. Oh well, how could they have known? When we got to the school, it was another story. Some of the sighted staff members began making comments about our canes.

Within an hour, I was told that Ms. Hernandez wanted to talk with me. I had no doubt what this was about. When I got to her office, she began quizzing me about my cane. She told me that a white cane was an international sign of blindness, and as I traveled, people would recognize the white cane and come to my assistance.

I replied, "That may be true, but I think that walking through Wal-Mart and knocking items off of shelves is an international sign of blindness." In addition to that, I told her that I was a state trooper, and if I wanted to carry a blue cane, I would.

Then she explained that I could not receive my certificate for completing the school if I didn't pass my classes and follow the rules. I asked her if I didn't get my certificate would that mean I wouldn't be able to be blind anymore. This did not help cool down our conversation. I tapped out of her office with my blue cane. She did not appreciate my sense of humor nor did she like my brashness.

I was a police officer, and was supposed to be the authority. I was the one who was to make decisions and direct others in what to do. I just couldn't leave that mentality behind.

About a week later, Sgt. Aubrey Futrell and Sgt. Vic Summers stopped by and asked me if I would be interested in going to Baton Rouge and doing a training video with the state police concerning my incident. They asked me if I was mentally and emotionally up to making this film. At first I was a little apprehensive. I had just started getting over some of the attacks and feelings from my shooting. Did I want to bring all that up again? Once I thought about it, I agreed, with the thought that maybe this film would keep some other officer from going through what I had to go through. They named the film *Incident on LA 15*.

Aubrey picked me up, and we rode to Baton Rouge together. It was a very enjoyable ride because we got to spend some time alone together. I told him that I now understood what he meant when I was in the academy, and I thanked him. I told him that I know if it had not been for the physical and mental training he had put me through, that I would have probably died right there on that highway.

The videotaping took all day long. My emotions and feelings about the shooting had been stirred. At least this time, I was able to complete sentences without breaking down and crying. Oh yeah, there were times that we had to stop, so I could regain my composure, but my state of mind was better than it had been a few months earlier. The videotaping went great, and I was glad that I had made that trip to Baton Rouge.

While we were driving back, Aubrey asked me if I would be interested in going to work at the state police training academy in Baton Rouge. I couldn't believe it! Maybe I was going to be able to still be a Louisiana State Trooper! Maybe not on the street, but I would do anything if I could only stay with the state police. I told him I would be ready tomorrow. He told me that I could move in with him and his wife. They had a spare bedroom, and I would be able to ride to work with him. I was more than happy, I was ecstatic! This was better than a dream come true!

I couldn't wait to get back to the school to share the news with Jonell. She would be graduating in one week, and she too was moving back home to New Mexico. We were both happy, but we were also very sad. She was a very special person in my life, and she would always be in my memory. She was the most courageous person that I had ever known. Parting was not as easy as I thought it would be, but it was time for us to move forward with our lives.

I've always been the type of person who finishes something when I start it, but I never did complete blind school. I learned a lot of things from there, but I didn't agree with some of their rules and procedures. The timing was right, and it was time to move on. Looking back, I'm glad that I went there, and I am especially glad that I met Jonell.

On September 30, 1986, I became a blind school dropout. That didn't bother me because I had a job to go to, and most of all, I was still going to be a Louisiana State Trooper.

VISIONS OF COURAGE

CHAPTER 30
"I DIDN'T TRAIN YOU TO QUIT"
Lt. Aubrey Futrell,
Louisiana State Police Training Academy

As an academy instructor, I was responsible for conducting the physical fitness testing for new recruits. Prior to their testing, each recruit was examined by the State Police physician. Bobby was summoned into the examination room. As he walked into the room, it was obvious that he was a former athlete, 5'11" approximately 180 pounds, broad shoulders, thick chest — what a specimen — all the way down to that right knee; which showed at least five scars on it.

As the doctor finished his examination, Bobby slid onto the table so that I could examine his knee. Twenty years ago I played football at Louisiana Tech University in Ruston, Louisiana, and was a trainer. I was used to seeing knees like this, but maybe not this bad. As I began to examine his knee, I noticed that there was hardly anything right about his knee. It was slack, there was no cartilage, and his ligaments had been repaired. You name it and it was wrong. I looked up at Bobby and told him that I didn't think he could get through the physical fitness part of the academy.

With those big brown eyes piercing back at me, he pleaded, "Aubrey, if you will just give me a chance, I will show you that I will make it. I am a competitive power lifter. I put strain on my knees everyday. If they can take that, surely, they can take the physical fitness of the academy." Although I had my reservations, I told him that I would let

191

him continue through the hiring process, but that he would have to sign a waiver stating that if his knee went out on him that he would have to resign as a state trooper, and he agreed.

Bobby was chosen as one of 55 cadets for the fall police academy. It was very obvious that he possessed leadership ability and was chosen by the other cadets as the class president.

I went to most of the Tech football games and one weekend while I was there, I ran into another trooper, Trooper Gary Crumpton, who was assigned to Troop F. Gary asked me how Bobby was doing, and I told him he was chosen as class president and doing fine. In jest, he told me that Bobby said that the physical fitness program at the state police was a sissy program and that anybody could go through it. We both chuckled because we knew no one in their right mind would say that because the state police physical fitness program was very rigorous.

The following Monday morning when all the cadets fell out for PT, I singled out Bobby to come to the front of the class. We were doing isometrics and proceeding into the hydro gym. The hydro gym room consisted of a dozen hydraulic machines, each designed to work a particular muscle. The machine could be programmed from light to extremely difficult. As Bobby stood in front of the class, surrounded by the hydraulic machines, I began to question him about what he had told Trooper Crumpton about the physical fitness program being a wimp program. He quickly denied that, so I called him a liar. "Are you calling a state trooper a liar?" I asked. Bobby quickly replied once again, "No, sir." This was a no win situation for him so he finally agreed that he had made those comments, although everyone knew that he had not.

I walked to each machine and programmed them for level six, the most difficult level. On that level, each repetition was like trying to push the wall away from you.

I turned to Bobby and said, "I'll show you a wimp program, and you can show the whole class what a wimp program this is." I pointed to the first machine and told Bobby to get started. I told him I wanted twenty repetitions on each machine.

At the sound of my whistle, Bobby began pumping out each rep and as soon as he was finished, he moved directly to the next machine and so on. I wondered, along with the class, how far he could go. It was not totally impossible, but eventually the body would go into oxygen deficit and no longer be able to push the weight. I learned a lot about Bobby that day, his determination, his desire, and his ability to never quit. He completed every machine, and when he finished, his face was pale from the lack of blood. His chest was heaving and pounding, and he struggled for his next breath, trying to regain oxygen in his body. I was impressed with his intestinal fortitude.

Half way through Bobby's academy class, I left to go to the FBI academy in Quantico, Virginia, and didn't see him again until after he graduated from the academy some seventeen weeks later. He had been assigned to Troop F in Monroe but was reassigned as a resident trooper in Tensas Parish. Over the next several years, I would only see Bobby periodically at the in-service training, at the academy in Baton Rouge. He was always the same, always laughing and joking.

It was a Sunday afternoon, and I was returning home to Baton Rouge from my parent's house in Jonesboro, Louisiana, when the news came on. The newscaster stated that Trooper Bobby Smith had been involved in a shooting the day before and was in stable condition but totally blind. He went on to say that Bobby had been shot in the face with a 12-gauge shotgun by a suspect after an altercation on a traffic stop. The suspect was killed, and Bobby Smith would be blind.

I recall the sick feeling in my stomach, and the thoughts of disbelief. Surely that must have been a mistake. After hearing the details, I began trying to put everything together. How could he have been shot in the face with a 12-gauge shotgun from 29 feet away? None of this made sense without all the facts. I began questioning myself – surely, I had covered all that in the academy. I know we talked about proper positioning in traffic stops and how to approach vehicles safely, didn't we? I began to try and blame myself. Didn't I teach Bobby all the things he needed to know so that this would never happen?

I called Troop F to confirm what I had just heard and learned to be true. Bobby had taken a shotgun blast to the face, at 29 feet, at 11:30 at night, and he was totally blind. I got back in my car and continued to drive wondering how Bobby was going to make it. He was so physically fit because he worked out on a regular basis. How in the world would Bobby deal with not being able to do all the things he had once done? A sense of sadness and feelings of doom surrounded me. I drove the rest of the way home in a daze.

I was sitting at a conference table, at the State Police Academy, with Sgt. Vic Summers and Sgt. Reggie Fleming discussing Bobby's shooting and trying to figure out what we could do to learn from the horrible incident. We decided that we would ask Bobby if he would help us recreate the shooting to see what he had done right, what he had done wrong, and how we could possibly learn from his mistakes so that others could possibly be saved.

THE BOBBY SMITH STORY

Vic, Reggie and I were at a retrainer in Monroe, and we decided to go by and see Bobby. We told him what we wanted to do, and he was in full agreement. During this time that we spent with Bobby, it was very obvious that he was still struggling emotionally in dealing with the shooting. The next week Trooper Mike Epps brought Bobby down to the State Police Academy in Baton Rouge so that we could shoot the film. We were going to title the tape, *Incident on LA 15, the Bobby Smith Shooting.*

Vic and I brought Bobby into the studio and began interviewing Bobby much like you would during an investigation. It was extremely obvious that after only a few minutes of Bobby telling his story, I realized exactly what kind of trauma he was still living in, while trying to deal with the aftermath of his shooting.

As I listened, he told about not only the shooting, but how he dealt with the shooting after four months — calling on his friends, family, and fellow officers to help him deal with the loss of his career, sight, and ultimately the loss of his wife. With that realization, I wanted to do more than tell the story of the shooting and how he had survived the shooting, but more importantly how he dealt with the trauma. After we had finished the interview with Bobby, we contacted all the troopers and deputies that were involved in the shooting, and one thing that we found out was, that everyone involved displayed symptoms of Post Traumatic Stress Disorder. They all had nightmares, flashbacks, fears of being shot, or of a fellow officer being shot, paranoia, stress, and depression.

After the film was completed, Bobby and I started traveling all across the state of Louisiana, some of Arkansas and Mississippi, showing the tape and talking about how we could help each other in dealing with the aftermath of violence. I told Bobby that there is a reason for everything that happens in life, and although I don't believe that God is personally responsible for all the tragedies in life, He can take those tragedies and turn them into something that can help others. Bobby and I had talked numerous times about my philosophy and about his shooting, as we were coming back from a lecture. The response we had received from this particular lecture was overwhelming. Many officers had come up with tears streaming down their faces and told us that they were much like Bobby. They too, thought they were like Superman, they had been well trained and nothing could ever happen to them. It was at this time that I knew in my heart this was the reason for the shooting. Bobby was a good trooper, and he was doing a lot more good by helping save other police officer's lives than he could have ever accomplished by just enforcing the law.

I will never forget the first seminar that Bobby and I did. I brought him in and seated him in the back of the class. Everyone just assumed that he was another police officer; they didn't know that he was blind. I gave my lecture and showed the film, *Incident on LA 15*. As the officers watched Bobby on that film tell about his shooting, you could see the impact that this had on them. But this was nothing compared to the impact of Bobby walking up to that podium and telling his story personally.

I walked Bobby to the podium and faced him toward the classroom. I described the room to Bobby so that he would know how far to look to the left and right and he began to talk. Except for Bobby's voice, a deathly silence fell over the whole room. I observed the faces of the officers, some with their mouths open, some with tears running down their faces. All attention was on Bobby. I thought to myself, this is the reason Bobby was shot.

THE BOBBY SMITH STORY

As Bobby concluded his lecture, the class stood to their feet and gave him a standing ovation. They then lined up and started making their way to the front to speak to us.

By word of mouth, we continued getting more speaking engagements, and all had these same responses.

VISIONS OF COURAGE

CHAPTER 31
LOUISIANA STATE TROOPER
ONCE AGAIN

I went to Baton Rouge and moved in with Aubrey and his wife. Captain Rutt Whittington was the director of the training academy. He and I met when he first took the position at the academy and we became friends. He thought it would be beneficial for the training academy if I did some work with Aubrey, due to my background in psychology and the personal experience I had in dealing with post traumatic stress. They put a desk in Aubrey's office for me, and I began working. They tried to make me feel like a part of the academy. I got some academy staff shirts just like all the other staff members. It was great to finally feel useful, but most of all I was still with the Louisiana State Police.

As time went on, I began to regain some of my self-confidence. It had been six months since the shooting and I was beginning to accept the fact that I was blind, and probably would be the rest of my life. Captain Whittington came to me one day and asked me if I would like to become a permanent part of the academy. Of course, I was ecstatic! My dreams were coming true! He told me that I would have to produce a proposal for Colonel Wiley McCormick, to let him know what I could do for the academy, and what my job would entail. In the short time that I had been there, I had learned that some from the upper line of the State Police were uncomfortable around me because I was a reminder of what could happen to any trooper. I knew that my proposal would have to be strong and convincing, but I knew I could do it.

Aubrey and I finally completed my proposal and set up an appointment to meet with the colonel. We had covered everything. On this particular day, Aubrey had scheduled me to speak to the new cadet class at the academy. I was in full uniform. My dream had already come true, for I was once again wearing that state police uniform. As I walked to the podium to speak to the class, I began remembering the days when I was a cadet. I had been chosen president of my class, and those feelings of being a new cadet ran through me. As I stood there, feelings of joy overcame me, tears began to flow down my face. This time the tears were from joy, not sorrow.

When I finished my presentation, it was time for my appointment with the colonel. I was still in full uniform, and my confidence was high after my presentation. I was ready for my meeting. We called ahead to let the colonel's secretary know that we were on our way, and she told us that he was expecting us.

When we arrived at headquarters, I got out and walked to the building using my cane. I had to prove that I was capable of doing things on my own, and I didn't need someone with me all the time. Aubrey knew I had to do this on my own, so he followed me. I tapped my way up the sidewalk, up the steps, into headquarters, and down the hall to the colonel's office.

As I waited to go into the colonel's office, I was very excited but also very afraid. Deep inside I knew that there was a possibility of rejection. The time had finally come; the colonel would see us now. We took a seat in his office and he sat behind his desk. He leaned back in his chair and began, "Now what's this meeting all about?" Captain Whittington has told me that you want to go to work at the academy instead of retiring." That killed my excitement and joy. I knew from the tone of his voice that this wasn't going to be a positive conversation.

I began to explain to him that I had been preparing myself mentally and physically to deal with the job, what my qualifications were, and the benefit that I thought I could be to the department. I handed him the proposal we had worked so hard on. It contained all the information he needed to inform him of everything that I could do for the state police training academy. It was typed neatly, in proper format, and placed in a manila envelope. He took the envelope from my hand, and I heard it slide across his desk. He didn't even open it. His chair squeaked as he leaned back.

"Bobby, let me be very honest with you," he said. "We've got the tape that you made for the academy, and we don't need you anymore." Those words were sharp daggers, and they pierced my heart. As I sat there, the tears began to roll down my face, and I thought, "I had given everything I had for the state police! All I wanted was to be a productive part of it! I had lost my eyesight in the line of duty, and this is what I got in return!"

I sat there, looking at him, not knowing what to say. He went on to tell me that he knew that I had contacted some very important people at Governor Edwin Edward's office in order to try and get help to stay on with them, but the state police procedure stated that to be an employee of the state police, you have to be sighted. I knew that procedure could have been changed with a stroke of the pen. Colonel Mc-Cormick also told me that he was not going to change the procedure and that I would not be assigned any more duties at the academy. He wished me well and informed me that he had already started the paperwork on my retirement.

I didn't know what to do. Should I have cursed him,

thanked him, or what? I knew what I wanted to do but not what was proper. I stood, excused myself and walked out. The colonel called Aubrey back into his office and began chastising him for even trying to pull a stunt like that.

When we left, we were very despondent. I wondered how could someone so heartless, with no empathy or compassion for anyone but himself, be in such a position of authority to control and dictate the way a person's life would go?

When we left headquarters, we went to Captain Whittington's office and told him what had happened. There I was, once again, riding that roller coaster of emotional turmoil. For the first time, I had been finally accepting myself as a blind person and was trying to form a normal life. Now this one person had taken from me, in less than fifteen seconds, what had taken me six months to build.

I continued to travel with Aubrey, telling my story and lecturing on officer survival, dealing with the aftermath of crime and violence, and post-traumatic stress. I began educating myself more and more on these topics, so I could help others.

One day I got a call from the secretary at Troop F. She told me that I needed to come there to sign my retirement papers. I asked her, "Why there? I live in Baton Rouge near headquarters. Why can't I sign my papers there?" Elaine told me that she didn't know why. The colonel had just called and said he wanted me to sign papers at Troop F, not headquarters.

Well, once more, I didn't have a choice, so I made arrangements for someone to drive me 230 miles to Monroe while Colonel McCormick and his photographer were flown up there in a helicopter. I guess he thought this was going to be some joyous occasion or something. We met at Troop

F and sadly, I signed my retirement papers. I could not believe the audacity of that man! He actually wanted to take a picture of me shaking his hand while he handed me my retirement papers. It was all just a big facade! They wanted the public to see how "gracious" the state police was being to that poor blind fellow. To say that I was furious was a gross understatement, but we'll leave it at that.

A few days later, I called headquarters and asked them when I would be getting my retirement watch since they had forced me to retire. They told me that I was not eligible for one. I couldn't believe it! How much longer would those people continue to snub me? They treated me like I was the criminal, but I was the victim! I wasn't the one who decided to go out one night and shoot a cop. I was the cop who was shot, and yet they rejected me as if I were a vagrant. I could not understand what horrible things I must have done as a state trooper that made me deserving of such treatment. I felt beaten and betrayed by the organization that I loved and cared for more than my own life. Not only had they turned their back on me, but now they were shooting the wounded.

When I returned from Monroe, Colonel McCormick had called Captain Whittington and told him that I needed to move out of Aubrey's office. I was no longer an employee, and I didn't belong there. It was just another act of their betrayal.

Since I still owned a house in Monroe, I decided to move back there and try to put my life together and decide what I would do. There wasn't any reason for me to stay in Baton Rouge any longer and I sure didn't want to, because it was just a painful reminder of what the state police had done to me. I had friends in Monroe, and I knew I could count on them.

Once I moved back into the house, the dragons came back to haunt me. I became very depressed. I still could not believe that someone could be so cruel. That one person had taken all my dreams and desires from me. There I was again sitting on my couch, my security blanket, sobbing uncontrollably. I couldn't stay there by myself, so I called Bobby Mann. Bobby heard the struggle in my voice. He knew that I was still trying to cope. He told me there was no reason for me to be at home by myself during the holiday season, feeling depressed. He asked me if I wanted to spend the holiday season with him and his family.

After staying with them, I decided that it would be a good idea to move back home to Alexandria, so I could be closer to my family. We needed each other's support. About a month after I had moved home, my family began introducing me to other people. My sister-in-law, Guinell, worked at the hospital and introduced me to some of the nurses there. Shortly after that, I began dating. It was really weird to go on a date and not know what they looked like. I guessed that all my dates would be blind dates. My family and friends were good to me because they always set me up with attractive women. I always wanted to have a mental picture of the different people that I met, so I would have someone describe them to me.

I was hesitant about going on dates. I worried that I might knock something over during dinner and that would have been so embarrassing. What if I had to go to the bathroom and the only person I was with was someone of the opposite sex? This was a whole new world of challenges.

I remember going to the theater one night with a young lady. We had dinner first, and it went pretty well. I didn't knock my water over, and I didn't even knock the waiter down when I walked through. Everything was going pretty well. After dinner we went to the show, and I really enjoyed myself. As a matter-of-fact, I had to tell her what was going on most of the time, instead of her describing the scenes to me. I had to go to the bathroom really bad though after the movie. She asked me if I thought I could find my way. I told her I thought I could but was afraid I might bump into someone at the urinal and that wouldn't be pleasant. I would really rather not. So she told me to wait a minute, and she would check in the women's bathroom. She checked, and there was no one in there. "Come on, hurry," she said. We walked in. She lead me to the stall and walked back out to stand guard at the door. I began using the bathroom when I heard her arguing with someone at the door.

"No, you can't go in," she said.

"Why can't I go in?" the person asked. "I've really got to go!"

"But you can't go right now," she repeated.

About that time, I heard the door opening. It was two giggling teenagers. They were laughing about that lady at the door that didn't want to let them in the bathroom. I didn't know what I was supposed to do. I finished very quickly and started out the door. As I was leaving, they were also coming out. They started screaming when they saw me.

"Oh no, now I'm going to get arrested for being in the woman's bathroom," I thought. My date, Charla, grabbed me by the arm and told me to come on before we got put in jail. We both laughed about it on the way home. She told me that this was by far, the most adventurous date that she had been on.

Several of the women that I dated seemed to get attached rather quickly to me. It wasn't necessarily in a romantic way but more in a "motherly" way. I guess they saw me as somewhat of a child at times, because I seemed to need their help all the time. They had to help pick out my clothes and set my table much like a mother would for her child.

It never failed. They always asked if it was true that if I felt their faces, I could tell what they looked like. I had always heard that all my life, but I guess since I was a blind school dropout, I never learned how to do that. I tried, but I never seemed to be able to tell what someone looked like by running my hands over their face. Oh well, if it was a pretty lady, I thought it was surely worth a try.

One thing that I learned about being blind was that a person's physical attributes were unimportant. I began to listen to a person from their heart. I learned about them from what they thought, said, and felt. Deep inside was where the true beauty was located. It was not on the outside, not how pretty her hair was, or how gorgeous her eyes were, or whether they were wearing stylish, expensive clothes. It was what came from the heart. I didn't enjoy being blind, but I was learning how to be a better person. I learned how to accept a person for who they were and not what they looked like.

After a few months of living with Danny and Guinell, I decided to move in with Betty. Betty was home everyday, and it helped me to have someone there with me all the time, to help me get my stuff done and someone to talk with when I needed to talk. We were very close, but there were times when I needed space. I needed some time alone to grieve over my losses, and she was sensitive enough to allow me that time. There were also times that I needed to talk and she would always be there to listen.

Sometimes she didn't understand what I was talking about; sometimes I didn't even understand. I really didn't know what was going on with me mentally.

THE BOBBY SMITH STORY

Being blind and living with Betty was really hard. It was hard on me, but I think it was even harder on her because she had to watch me struggle with every single day. She had to watch me while I tried to pick out my clothes, move through the living room without running into the coffee table, and trying to keep from knocking things over. She was very understanding as she witnessed my frustrations every day. I was still dealing with so much unprocessed anger and unforgiveness. I could not forgive myself for the mistakes I made, nor for getting shot in the first place.

Sometimes I took my anger out on her. I had always heard that we usually lash out at the ones closest to us. In this case, that old adage was absolutely true. The closest person to me at that time was Betty, and she was doing all that she could for me. She supported me, laughed and cried with me, and listened to me when I needed to dump some water out of my glass, but I always seemed to take out my anger on her. I hated that, but I just couldn't seem to stop myself.

I was trying so hard to survive, mentally and emotionally. I felt like I was treading water in a deep ocean. Every now and then my head would go under, and I would have just enough strength to pull it out and tread just long enough to catch my breath before I went back down again. I was emotionally bankrupt.

I remember one morning when Betty and I were paying my bills. She wrote out all my checks and put them in envelopes for the mail. We got ready to go to town to get some groceries. I depended on her for everything and I didn't want to admit it, but at that time, Betty had become my servant.

We had left the house and had gotten about three or four miles down the road when I asked Betty if she had picked up my envelopes. She said, "I handed them to you, so you must have laid them down." I thought to myself that she was right, I did lay them down, but it was just easier to blame her.

I yelled, "Why didn't you pick them up?"

She replied, "But Bobby, I thought you had them."

"I can't believe you didn't see them sitting on the table! You know I had to get that in the mail today! It has to be there tomorrow! You know how important that was! I can't believe you just left them on the table! What's wrong with you?"

Betty burst into tears as a result of my angry tirade. Through her sobbing she said, "Bobby, I'm doing the best that I can." Then I felt like such a jerk. We weren't used to all this blindness stuff, and it had begun to take its toll.

She didn't say another word, and it broke my heart. Then I started crying. I was crying for her more than anything else. I had so many different emotions coming at me from different directions. I was furious about the loss of my sight, career, and marriage. I didn't know how to deal with all of those emotions. I leaned over and gave her a hug and asked her to forgive me. I knew that she did, because she always did. Everyone should be as fortunate as I to have such a wonderful sister.

I had been living with her for several months when I told her that I was thinking about building a house right down the street. Terry was a contractor, and I knew he could help me build it. Betty thought that it was a good idea, so we agreed to talk with Terry. When I called Terry, he told me that he knew the people that owned the lots down the street from Betty and that he would build my house. I was excited about the prospect of building a new home. It would be a brand new place for me to start all over again. A new house, in a new town, maybe things were finally beginning to look up.

I had always wanted a two-story house, with a bedroom upstairs and a loft overlooking the den. Terry knew exactly what I wanted and drew up the plans. We started building immediately, and I was ecstatic! I had been an electrician when I got out of high school and had wired houses before. I asked Betty if she would help me wire the house. And we did. Once again, I began to regain my self-confidence. I began to think that maybe I could do some of the things that I had done in the past. Maybe I couldn't be a policeman anymore, but surely I could go on with my life. I wondered, "What are they paying blind electricians these days?" I realized that I had just lost my sight, not my mind.

Betty and I chose the necessities for my house. She did everything for me. We also went shopping for the furniture. Boy, was that something. I turned my sister loose with my checkbook. She really enjoyed that! She picked out living room, bedroom and dining room furniture. At last, the house was finished, and I moved in.

It felt pretty good to be spending the first night in my new home. I had a new house and a new beginning. I had started going back to the same church I had grown up in, Philadelphia Baptist Church. I had accepted Christ, as my Savior, in that same church 22 years earlier. At this time, I made a commitment to God. I committed myself to serve Him and become a better person. I became active in my church and community, and my life began to slowly slip into a familiar routine.

One day, I was with my brother at the barbershop. As I was sitting in the chair, talking with the barber, I heard someone walk up. I heard a very familiar voice of an old friend. This was a voice that I hadn't heard in over a year and a half. It was Rutt Whittington.

He was from the Alexandria/Pineville area, and his dad was a professor of Religion at Louisiana College. Rutt had been promoted to Major of Region III Headquarters in Alexandria for the State Police.

"Bobby, how are you doing?" he asked.

"I'm doing fine, Major," I replied. "How are you?"

He said that he was doing really good and told me about his new job at the Region.

I told him that I had just been sitting around at the house and trying to figure out what I needed to do with the rest of my life.

Rutt said for me to come by and see him one day because he needed to talk to me.

I went by the Major's office, and as always, he was very helpful and courteous. He was a very empathic man. He asked me if I would like to move out to the Region and hang out with some of the troopers. They would love to have me around.

"How are you going to do that?" I asked. "As you recall, Colonel McCormick has made it pretty clear that I am not welcome on state police property. I guess I am just too much of a reminder."

"We'll cross that bridge if we ever get there," he replied.

The next day, I got Betty to take me to Major Whittington's office at the Region III headquarters. After a few casual pleasantries, he walked me down the hall and introduced me to some of the guys. I met Sgt. Steve Barretts first. I remembered meeting Steve at tactical unit training. Everyone knew him. He was a comedian, very quick witted and always had something to say. We walked into his office, and the Major introduced me.

"Steve, this is Bobby Smith," he said. "He was the trooper that was shot and blinded in Winnsboro." Steve recalled that occasion. The Major began telling Steve that I would be doing some peer counseling for the State Troopers Association and that I would be using one of the desks at the Region.

"Oh, that's great Major. Of all the people that I have to supervise now, all I need is to have to take care of a blind man. I'm not going to have to hold his hand in the bathroom, am I?" he asked.

We all started laughing. I didn't exactly know how to take Steve at first. We became very good friends, for we had several things in common. We were both raised on farms with cows, horses and the whole nine yards, a real Old McDonald's Farm.

One day he invited me to his house in the country. Steve, his wife, Claudia, and their three children took me in as a member of their family. I was doing a great deal of speaking engagements during this time.

I was sitting in Steve's office one day, and Aubrey Futrell called. He asked how I was doing because he hadn't seen me in a while. I told him what the Major was doing for me at the Region, and how good it made me feel to just hang around with some of the guys from the state police. He then told me that he had just gotten a call from the director of the American Law Enforcement Society in Wisconsin. They wanted me to be the guest speaker at their first annual banquet in New Orleans.

"Can you do it?" Aubrey asked.

I assured him that it would not be a problem since I didn't have a permanent job.

Aubrey and I went to New Orleans and I did the speaking engagement. It was probably one of the largest

211

groups of officers I had ever spoken to. The lecture was less than great, but I told my story and how I had to deal with the aftermath of that violent attack. Everyone there was a police trainer, and I tried to give them some information they could take back to their department and pass on to their officers. After this engagement, I started getting more and more calls to come and tell my story. At first it was just Louisiana, but calls began coming from Mississippi, Alabama, Arkansas, Texas, and as far as Oklahoma. My circle of speaking was getting larger and larger. "Things must be looking up," I thought. Once again, I began to feel more confident. Maybe there was a reason I was shot. Maybe it happened so I could try and help save other police officer's lives through my speaking. I began thinking that maybe I could help them find some answers.

I tried desperately to make the best out of a bad situation.

CHAPTER 32
THE B.A.D.G.E

My brother, Terry, owns a contracting business, and had built me a house. I moved into that house, and was going through my big walk-in closet in my bedroom. As a blind person, my hands become my sight to a certain extent. I was going through my closet looking for a particular shirt. I was going down stairs to work out, and I had this certain shirt that I was going to work-out in. It was an old ragged shirt, and I remembered hanging it up in my closet. Feeling through that closet, I am thinking, "That's not it," and I came across a very familiar shirt. It was my Louisiana State Police shirt. I began to feel the shirt, and I came across the patch on the right sleeve. I pulled the shirt off and sat on the floor and began to cry because I knew that I would never wear that shirt again. I could put it on and walk around with my uniform, badge, and everything, as much as I wanted to, but I could never ever truly wear that shirt again.

Sitting there, I ran my hands across the front of that shirt feeling my tactical unit patch, my ribbons, and my cross pins in my pocket. I ran across something very familiar to me. It was my gold badge which was in the shape of a boot, the shape of Louisiana. Across the top it says, Trooper Louisiana State Police. In the center there is a blue and white state seal which says, "Union, Justice, Confidence". Our state bird is a pelican, and there is a female pelican in there feeding her young. As I was sitting on the floor, I ran my hand across that badge and the tears began to drip on the back of my hands. I cried because I knew that a mistake

213

that I had made in being arrogant and in a hurry to make an arrest, which was totally asinine, would cause me to never wear that uniform again.

As I sat there in the closet feeling that shirt and badge, much like the hallucination that I had from the football game the night I got shot, I had another hallucination. I saw five letters appear before me in my dark world. In front of me in that closet was the five letters B.A.D.G.E . I don't know where this came from, and I'm thinking, is this another hallucination? What's going on? Is this from God? Is this divine intervention and where is this from? I saw it - B.A.D.G.E , these five big black bold letters. At that time I began to think about that badge and what it meant to me.

The "B" stands for *Bravery*. Much too often we are called upon to perform acts of bravery. If you look at Webster's dictionary, it says bravery is acting in the presence of fear. We all know that there are times that we are scared to death in law enforcement, or we better have enough sense to be afraid. There are times that we should know whether to stay or run. There are times to run. But we have to be brave, and I thought about it as I sat there in that closet. Many incidents that I had gone on, I was scared to death. Searching a house that we knew a suspect was hiding in, scared me to death. You can not eliminate fear in every situation. I recalled an incident where I worked a fatality accident, and when I got there, the ambulance was there. As I pulled up, this lady was hysterical. I saw a body covered up. I later found out that it was a ten-year-old little girl. My daughter, at the time, was eight years old. As I got out of the car I'm thinking, "I'm the State Trooper. I'm here to protect and serve and they look to me for help." I got out of the car, and she started walking towards me and our eyes met. I could feel the tears rolling up in my eyes. I'm thinking that

I can't deal with this because all I can think of is my own child. I turned away quickly and started back to my car, and I reached in, acting like I was getting some reports off of my seat. When in essence, I was giving myself time to regain my composure. I wiped my face and cleared my throat, then walked back out there. As I started back out there to get the essential information for my report, she started running towards me again. I couldn't take it anymore because she was saying, "Please help me. Please." There was nothing that I could do, but we embraced and she sobbed. Tears were streaming down my face, and I'm thinking, "Is this what it is all about, just helping, not writing tickets or making arrests? Being there for one another." We have to be brave.

The "A" stands for *Attitude*. Much too often we get into this negative mentality that the world is out to get us. I'm a firm believer in this "garbage in, garbage out." If you're thinking about garbage in the negative world, then you're saying it. No one likes to be around a complainer all the time. I was doing a lecture one day at a recruit school, and told my story about my shooting and how I returned fire. During the break, I overheard two new recruits saying "I'll tell you one thing, if that had been me, I would have fired my six shots and quickly reloaded. I would not have gone down with just one shot." I got angry. They were not there and don't know what they would have done in the same situation. We get this tough, negative attitude that gets us into a lot of trouble. That's not what our badge is about. It's about a positive attitude and about caring for one another.

The "D" stands for *Dedication*. No one is forced to be a policeman. If you are not dedicated to your agency that you work for, you need to leave. I would gladly change places with you and not complain. I never complained before my shooting. I loved being a cop. For 10 years I loved

215

and was committed to being the best cop that I could be.

The "G" stands for *God*. I am not going to push my beliefs on anyone. These are my personal beliefs. I believe that there is a God. I believe that he did have a son named Jesus Christ that died on the cross for me. I believe someday that we will have to answer to God for what we have done. The Bible says that you are ordained by God to be the centurions to enforce the law of the land. The Bible also says it is a calling. God doesn't care about the authority of police officers here on earth. God is the supreme authority.

The "E" stands for *Empathy*. The police say that they are there for each other, but that's the biggest lie I have ever heard. There are too many police officers out there hurting mentally, emotionally, and crying out for help. If my friends in law enforcement hurt, I hurt. I read a story about a young sixteen-year-old girl who had a blood disorder. She had to have a blood transfusion or she would die. They went to the doctor and ran all the tests to determine what could be done to save her life. No one in her family matched her blood. Her parents were in the doctor's office one day looking at some blood results. Their 16 year-old daughter and her 8 year-old brother Billy were with them. The doctor walked in and asked who the little boy was. The parents said, "This is our youngest son." The doctor wanted to test the boy, and the parents agreed. The doctor knelt down in front of the little boy and asked, "Billy, do you understand that if your sister does not get some blood she is going to die?"

Billy said, "Yes, I understand that." The doctor told the little boy that he wanted to test his blood to see if it matched and if it did, could his sister have some? The boy said sure! They took him in, tested his blood and sure enough, it matched. They hooked them up for the transfusion. When they finished the transfusion, the doctor came in for a moment and took the girl out for some tests. The little boy was left in the room by himself momentarily. When the doctor came in, the little boy's lips were quivering, and tears were rolling down his face. The doctor asked Billy if he was all right. Billy shook his head yes, and the doctor asked him what was wrong. "Why are you crying? Are you hurting?"

After a few minutes, Billy sits up and begins to talk to the doctor. The doctor again asks Billy why he is crying. Billy says, "Doctor, when am I going to die?" The doctor tells him that he is not going to die. He lets the little boy know they just took some of his blood to give to his sister and that he is going to be all right. The little boy thought that when he gave his blood that he would die. The doctor asked Billy a question. He said "Billy, in thinking that you would die, why did you give your sister some of your blood?" Billy said, "Don't you understand...she's my sister and I love her."

As I sat there in that closet, watching the letters BADGE in front of me, the G and E separated themselves from the word and moved away. I remembered my head moving and following the G and E to the right side of the closet. I'm looking at G and E to the right and in front of me is BAD. Wondering what's happening, I realize what I'm seeing. Show me a police officer that wears that badge who does not have God and empathy for his fellow citizen and I will show you what is left: A bad cop. Some cops, like myself, have put their jobs before their family. Your family should be your number one priority. When you put your job before your family, you will lose that relationship with your family. Don't miss out on your children's life. They need you to be there for them all of the time.

My daughter was 22 years old when I buried her. I cannot go back and build those memories again. Please do not wait until it's too late to spend time with your children. I do not have that option anymore. Your family is the most important thing you will ever have, not your job. You're not guaranteed that they will be here tomorrow. I miss my daughter tremendously. My only comfort in this is that I know she is in heaven and that one day we will be together again for eternity. If I have said at least one thing in this book that would make you a better person, then it's worth being in this dark world that I live in. I would rather be the guy I am today living in total darkness, than the person I was 19 years ago with 20/20 eyesight. It is my goal and objective for you today to be able to see as well as I do.

CHAPTER 33
"HOW I FELL IN LOVE WITH SOMEONE WHO COULD NOT SEE ME"
By Janie Smith

I met Bobby truly by God's design and in His time. As a young teen, I can remember lying awake at night, saying my prayers and asking God to let me see into the future, by way of a dream, who I would one day marry. Back then, I did not receive any clue about my future mate. I don't know how I would have responded if I had been given the information that I would marry, divorce and then marry a blind man. In my latter teen years, I turned away from God and decided to live life my way. I dropped the "mate" issue with God and went about my own business regarding dating relationships.

Bobby and I met when I was 28 years old. By then, I had dated so many men looking for love in all the wrong faces and places that my heart had been broken and stomped on repeatedly. In addition, I was recovering from an extremely abusive marriage that had ended in divorce and had left my heart and soul shattered. It was shortly after that time in my life that I was introduced to Bobby by his cousin, Sonya Prestridge. She and I were co-workers in the Food Service Department at St. Francis Cabrini Hospital in Alexandria, Louisiana.

I worked as a clinical dietitian at the hospital in 1988. Until this point in my life, I had not been very selective about either male or female friends. After all I had been through, I became determined not to use the same poor judgment with people that I had in the past. I decided to befriend and date only people who were *sincere* Christians. So, at the hospital, I looked for Christian co-workers with which to establish friendships. Sonya was one of two sincere Christians I found who was genuinely "sold out" to Jesus. Later, I discovered that the other Christian woman was Bobby's Aunt Euna Rae Burnaman.

One day, during a lunch break with Sonya, she told me about her cousin, Bobby, whom she loved very much. Sonya said that she would like for us to meet if I would agree. I remember how she told me, bit by bit, many wonderful things about Bobby. The more Sonya described him, the more excited I got about the possibility of meeting a decent man who really loved and served God. However, she saved the fact that he was blind for the very end of the conversation. I was surprised when she told me that, but I then told her, "Well, I dated just about every other kind of man, why not a blind man, especially if he loves the Lord?"

While I was recovering from past abusive relationships, I was given a prayer by my best friend, Sue Ellen Blackburn. She was a preacher's daughter as well as a tremendous Christian woman with great compassion and wisdom. Many days I poured my heart out to her, and she loved me unconditionally. One day, she gave me a copy of a prayer called, "A Prayer for Your Future Mate," that was given to her by her mother when Sue Ellen had prayed for her Christian husband.

During the next three weeks, I began praying that special prayer every night and talked once again with God about a Christian mate. During my prayer times, I admitted and confessed to God that I had made so many mistakes, regarding dating, relationships and my first marriage. I told God that I no longer trusted my judgment when it came to men and that if it was *His Will* for me to marry that *He* would have to choose the man for me and then tell me, specifically, Himself.

In addition to praying the special prayer, I completely surrendered my life to God. I realized that His will was really in my best interest, and after so many mistakes, I relented and gladly let Him be Lord of my life. I spent quite a bit of time crying before God, telling Him that my heart's desire was to marry and to have a family, but only if it was His will. I remember telling Him, "If it is not Your will for me to marry again, or if You'd like me to be a missionary in Africa, then that will be O.K. too." Back then I thought being a missionary in Africa was the worst thing to be called by God to do. My lack of spiritual maturity kept me from seeing the good of being called to a situation like that. In spite of my spiritual immaturity, God knew my heart, for this was the first time in a long time that I trusted God with my future.

It wasn't long before Sonya arranged a meeting for Bobby and me. A friend of Bobby's, Steve Barrett, who was a Louisiana State Trooper, was having back surgery at the hospital where we worked, and Bobby was planning to visit Steve while he was there. When Bobby arrived at the hospital, I scheduled a work break and went with Sonya to meet him in Steve's room. Sonya introduced me to Bobby and Steve, and then left. Bobby was sitting on a bay window bench in the room and invited me to sit by him. I felt awkward and nervous about meeting him, but he had a mysterious way of comforting me with his words and a delightful sense of humor. During the conversation, he asked me to describe my appearance and what I was wearing. As the meeting progressed, we got to know each other and enjoyed each other's company as we laughed and joked. However, during this time of excitement and joy for us, Steve was watching in pain, from his hospital bed while recovering from back surgery. Later, we all reflected back on this scene and chuckled about how Steve's pain and misery ironically provided a setting and opportunity in which we first met and began to fall in love.

During my initial conversation with Bobby, I learned that I had had several misconceptions about him, concerning his blindness. When he asked me to go to the movies with him, I asked him if blind people went to the movies. He said, "Heck, yes!" Then he asked me if I would like to go eat at a seafood restaurant. Little did he know that movies and seafood were two of my favorite things!

The time I spent with Bobby that day went by very quickly, but I had to get back to work, so I told him that my break was over. He made one last request before I left. He asked me if he could hold my hand for a moment. I extended my hand, like a flat handshake, and rested it in his hand, and he held it for several seconds. I thought to myself, "I guess this is how blind people communicate – through touch." Then I said to Bobby, "Good - bye. I'll give you a call later to confirm the plans," and turned and walked away.

Just as I was passing through the doorway, I so clearly heard God's voice in my inner being say, "He's the *One*!" In shock, I swung back around abruptly and glared at Bobby in sheer astonishment. Steve still says that he can remember the look I gave Bobby and how he described my look to Bobby when I left the room. Bobby couldn't see my expression that day and perhaps, if he would have been able to, it might have scared him away.

As I walked down the hospital corridor, I could hear Bobby and Steve talking about me in the distance. I began talking frantically with God about what I had just heard Him say. My conversation with God went something like this,

"God, you can't be serious about Bobby being the one for me — a blind person! You know I don't work well with the blind and handicapped!   Lord, that was Jeanie, my twin sister, who worked each summer at the Lion's Club Crippled Children's Camp — not me! I can't handle a handicapped person! Besides that, he's overweight, and you know how I feel about weight and nutrition! He's got a beard, and I think beards are so unattractive, and besides that, he's got a large fake eye that looks weird! I know he is a Christian, but what about the blindness?"

During the next couple of days, I thought about my past worldly, superficial views and values. I remembered that when I selected my first mate, I used physical appearance, money-making potential and prestige as the most important criteria. None of those things were sufficient to hold a marriage together for a lifetime nor could they make any amount of abuse worth taking. I learned the hard way what was really important in selecting a mate. In my past relationships, there had been so much emphasis placed on my physical appearance for my sense of worth and acceptance. I was not allowed to go out in public without first being made up from head to toe. I spent hours in front of a mirror trying to reach perfection on the outside while masking great emotional pain on the inside. I knew firsthand about the hurt associated with being someone's show piece, but unfortunately, I had learned to treat others in the same cruel way.

After I heard from God about Bobby being my future mate, I became afraid, and needless to say, I did not call him back to confirm our dating plans. Although God had answered my prayer and gave me the specific direction about a mate, the fear I felt about being married to a blind person set into motion various conscious and subconscious sabotaging efforts concerning this relationship. Despite of my internal struggle, God was still in control of our relationship.

After a few days, Bobby called me and politely asked me why I had not called him back as I said I would. He must have sensed my apprehension, but he continued to pursue the dating plans we had tentatively agreed upon that day at the hospital. Once again, I was charmed by him and agreed to go out with him.

The evening we went on our first date, I was running late and decided to send my identical twin sister, Jeanie, in my place to meet Bobby and his twin sister, Betty, as a prank. Later, he discovered the truth about who Jeanie was when they came by to get me. He had a good sense of humor and took the "twin switching" joke well. Jeanie and her husband, Frank, went out with us and that evening was the beginning of the rest of my life. We went to dinner at an all-you-can-eat seafood buffet in Turkey Creek and then went to see a bizarre science fiction movie. That movie was nearly impossible for me to describe to Bobby in many of the scenes, but we laughed heartily at my efforts.

We still enjoy going to movies and eating seafood. However, many times, instead of my describing movie scenes to any great extent, he instead, contends with my questions, "What did they say? Who did it?" Many times he is better able to follow a movie than I am due to his heightened perceptions and excellent listening skills. As far as restaurants are concerned, the local all-you-can-eat seafood restaurant, "Jarrell's," located in Monroe, is Bobby's favorite place to eat, and the people who work there know us on a first-name basis.

Getting back to my first date with Bobby, at about ten o' clock that evening, Jeanie and Frank went home. Bobby invited me to go to his house for coffee and conversation. That night we shared our life stories as he held me in his arms on his lap as he rocked me gently and respectfully in his large, blue recliner chair. It seemed like I was in heaven then, because I felt sincere love in his touch, just as he said he felt from me from the holding of my hand in the hospital the first day we met. He explained that what he felt in the touch of my hand helped him sense the beauty of my heart.

That first night out with Bobby, I experienced such great communication with him because he sincerely cared about hearing what I had to say. He could hear my words, as well as the emotional tone of my voice down to the depths of my soul. We talked for hours and even discussed the subjects of marriage and children on the first date!

I believe that God keeps His Word, and he can restore what the locust destroyed at light speed. Bobby, like no other man in my life, could truly see through my exterior and into my heart and know me. This was one of many reasons I fell in love with him.

We were married on September 7, 1988, just three short months after we met. What about his physical appearance, which I was initially so concerned about? Well, he shaved the beard soon after we began dating when he learned about my opinion of them. Even now he remains very considerate of my preferences. Then, as time went on, we talked about health, exercise and nutrition. I discovered that he was sincerely interested in good health and had given his best efforts at following a competitive weight lifter's diet for years, but he had so much misinformation. He wanted to follow a healthy eating plan for an athlete but needed assistance. So, we developed a well-balanced diet that was better suited to his preferences and physical needs. He soon lost weight, but more importantly, he was better able to manage his condition of hypoglycemia (low blood sugar) and the episodes of emotional eating he had been having due to the amount of stress he had been under.

Now, about his oversized, prosthetic eye. He did not know that the eye was unattractive; well-meaning friends and family had seen him suffer so much that they were afraid of hurting his feelings by telling him it looked bad. However, after talking with his ever-so-blunt friend, Steve Barrett and myself about his prosthesis, Bobby went back to New Orleans and had his eye properly fitted with a prosthesis that was more pleasing in appearance.

With some time and love, we both got healthier on the inside and the outside. However, an important lesson I learned from Bobby was how to first love from the inside out, and what may or may not exist on a physical level is of low priority in comparison to the condition of the heart of a person.

Bobby is my big, strong "Angel Teddy Bear" who loves me for who I am, and I am able to return the same, unconditional love to him. He gave me the nickname of "The Angel With a Broken Wing," when we first met. Now, I am his "Angel" who God has healed both heart and soul through God's love and through the gift of Bobby's love to me.

When we were first married, I had several disorganized and absent - minded habits, such as kicking off my heels and leaving them around the house, leaving drawers and cabinet doors open, leaving glass beverages on the end of counter tops, and generally not putting things in their appropriate places. My totally visual and sloppy world merely presented an aesthetic problem for myself when I lived alone. This was a problem I tolerated well and corrected it when I felt like it. However, in my new, shared world with Bobby, habits or conditions like these created danger zones for him and often resulted in falls, bruises, bloody noses, gashes across his forehead, as well as many broken glasses and a great deal of pain, aggravation and frustration — especially for Bobby.

I remember one incident in the kitchen when I was loading the dishwasher. He could hear the noise but was unaware of what I was doing and he tried to get by. Well, his sudden reaction to tripping over the open door required a tremendous amount of coordination to prevent him from breaking any bones – especially his neck! He performed quite an acrobatic feat while stumbling and practically flying over the door. Thankfully, he was not seriously hurt, but we were both scared by the incident and realized that I had a great deal to learn about living with a blind husband. Basically, living with him meant that I had to learn to be more aware of others and their needs as well as how to be a much more organized homemaker. God knew that I needed some improvement in these areas anyway.

You may be wondering if I expend a tremendous amount of effort cleaning and keeping things in order. I don't. Bobby is the kind of husband I believe that most women pray for because he is extremely energetic and helpful with chores and responsibilities around the house. He does laundry, dishes, ironing, makes beds, sweeps and mops floors, cleans bathrooms, vacuumes and even cooks quite well. At first, I thought that he was handicapped and needed someone to take care of him. If the truth be known, in our case, it is Bobby who takes care of me! I believe that God knew all of this, as well as my dislike of domestic chores, and decided to bless me with Bobby. Many times I describe him to others as an independent blind person, and to those of us that know him, that is just what he is – an independent blind person.

Although he functions very well doing a variety of activities, he is not able to drive a car well. This limitation is managed with many helpful friends. I thank God for them.

There are many funny stories I could share about my inability to read a map when we first began traveling for Bobby's speaking engagements. To my surprise, that problem was remedied by his navigating expertise. He is a walking - talking road map. Bobby is able to recall many directions and reach many destinations without reading a map, due to his experience working as a state trooper. He is also able to excellently obtain and recall verbal directions.

When we were first married, road trips were quite interesting and at times, extremely frightening and frustrating. When I first began driving, we would get lost sometimes, and I would panic. However, during the panicky moments when neither of us knew which way to go on some back road late at night, I remember how he took on the role of an advisor and encourager and how he helped me calm down so that I could think clearly.

With a sense of awe, I have come to greatly respect his wisdom and ability to love others and meet other people's needs. His blindness provides opportunities for myself and others to develop and/or discover new or hidden strengths and abilities. These strengths are often discovered in and through the initial guise of helping him. His blindness acts as a great teacher. It has a way of drawing out abilities and developing competencies which may not have been apparent or otherwise utilized.

With nearly ten years of extensive driving experience, my driving and navigating skills have greatly improved, and I don't get lost nearly as frequently! Also, during these past ten years, Bobby has required a great deal of air transportation due to an increasing demand for his public speaking and police training skills. He travels extensively across the United States and abroad. He has surpassed the need for my driving abilities, and I often stay home and assume child-care responsibilities when he is away. I am very proud of his incredible courage and speaking abilities.

One of my concerns when I first married him was of his ability to provide an income. I did not know what he would end up doing or how he would develop a new career. He was studying for a master's degree in counseling/psychology when I met him. However, his love for police work never ceased. By the work and grace of God, I have watched Bobby through the years develop a new career in law enforcement in the area of public speaking and training.

I didn't know what he was going to do with his future. I considered his blindness to be a serious limitation, and I didn't know what his future job abilities or possibilities could be. This presented me with another opportunity to learn how to trust God in the area of finances and careers. There were many days that I fretted about whether or not the money we needed would be available to us without having to make serious hardship changes.

Early in our marriage, I brought my money-worrisome soul to Bobby, who most of the time, graciously listened to my-way-of-the-world perspective on finances. I remember when I first took over the financial records. I started out writing checks for tithes and offerings to various groups, following his past pattern of expenses. I remember asking him what this was all about and requesting that we stop giving so much money away, especially since we had no guaranteed source of income other than his State Police retirement. We had lots of bills, and were at the mercy of whatever calls or requests we could get for his speaking. At this point, giving to God or others made no sense to me with my worldly view of finances. That's when Bobby began teaching me about how to totally trust God. I had surrendered other areas of my life to God, but when it came to money, I had much to learn.

One day, I delivered one of my fretful money discourses to Bobby, that ended in tears for me and frustration for him. He kept telling me, "Don't worry, God will take care of us!" This was his response to all of my financial concerns. I was baffled, at my wit's end, and his beliefs and practices of tithes and offerings just did not seem to make sense in the face of our bills and an extremely variable source of income. I had great difficulty grasping this spiritual truth, and I continued to have despairing thoughts and emotions concerning a lack of funds. Two days following our conflict, we checked the mail and discovered eight envelopes that contained checks, totaling approximately $3,000. As I opened each piece, I screamed with joy and excitement as well as praises to God! Bobby just laughed at my child-like antics. I screamed as though I was a game show participant. I knew then, that this was what he meant when he said that God would take care of us. I thank God for this "hands-on" experience.

Throughout the past ten years, my faith in God concerning finances has greatly increased. He has always provided the finances we needed. I am grateful to God for Bobby's example of faithfulness in giving. To my amazement and to God's glory, Bobby continues to obtain multiple requests to speak to various organizations and in doing so, is able to provide for our family. I have attended many of his speaking engagements and have heard and experienced his charisma and knowledge, on many topics, for the purpose of teaching and motivating. God has given Bobby an extra dose of wisdom and a phenomenal talent for public speaking. I now know who is in charge of our income, as well as Bobby's career — God.

THE BOBBY SMITH STORY

Bobby is a brilliant man with incredible courage and perseverance. One example of this was his decision to pursue a graduate degree in exercise physiology at Northeast Louisiana University(NLU), which led us to Monroe, Louisiana, in 1990. During this time, I was a new mother with a six-week-old baby boy.

Now let me tell you about the gift of a beautiful son that God blessed us with on February 12, 1990. His name is Brad Elliott Smith. He is 12 years old at the writing of this book. Family members have said that it looks like Bobby just spit Brad right out of his mouth. Yes, he does look just like Bobby, and I know why. Before and during my pregnancy, I prayed that if it was God's will for us, that I would like to have a son and that I would like him to look just like Bobby. God gave me the desires of my heart. Watch out what you pray for, because you just might get it!

While studying as a full-time graduate student, Bobby worked full-time at the West Monroe Police Department in physical fitness and training and also worked as a graduate student in the university fitness laboratory, which covered the cost of his tuition. He studied by recording notes on audio tapes and then listening to the lectures over and over again. He also hired people to read and assist him with research. Bobby's exams were given to him orally by his professors.

To be admitted into graduate school, Bobby had to complete the Graduate Record Examination(GRE), and he did so orally for eight hours. By the way, I took the same exam in the usual written fashion, and Bobby's scores were higher than mine! But I wasn't the only one beat by a blind man.

As Bobby studied and completed his course work at the university, he gained the reputation of setting the curve in his classes. Being blind did not mean he was dumb by any means. Within two years, he completed his master's degree with a 3.9 grade point average!

Just as he achieved academic excellence at the university, he has earned and continues to earn a great deal of admiration and respect at our home as a husband and a father. The term "Fatherhood" and Bobby Smith go very well together. From the time Brad was born, Bobby has been intimately involved with the rearing of our son. There were many nights that Bobby held and rocked Brad when Brad was unable to rest because he had chronic ear, nose and throat infections. He had two surgeries to correct these problems before he was two years old. It was a difficult time for all of us.

I knew Bobby was an excellent rocker from my experience with him on our first date, when he held and rocked me in his arms so lovingly and tenderly. Now, Brad who had many sleepless and restless nights, needed Bobby's comfort and love. Many mornings, I found Brad resting contentedly on Bobby's chest, and both of them were fast asleep in the recliner. I thank God for Bobby's willingness to help. When Brad was a toddler, and even sometimes now when he wakes up in the middle of the night, he calls out for his daddy. He is a very smart child and learned from an early age that his daddy wakes up much more pleasant than his mother.

Bobby and Brad have such a beautiful, loving, father-son relationship. Brad adores his daddy and is learning how to be a compassionate servant of God just like him. Bobby's blindness is a teacher, like none other, for all of us. We have prayed for his eyes to be healed and are still believing for that healing. However, in the meantime, we are continually learning what it is to live by God's grace and to be patient and to trust God no matter what. Love has no boundaries and can reach far beyond the physical realm of seeing.

THE BOBBY SMITH STORY

Bobby was always willing to help care for Brad, in any way that he could, even with such a thing as a dirty diaper. One day I went to the store, and Bobby was left to care for Brad. When I returned, I found the two of them and Brad's room a stinky mess. Bobby had given his best effort at changing a loaded diaper. Brad was not a calm baby and had rambunctiously kicked and rolled while being changed. He did not make any concessions for Bobby's blindness. Although I did not like the mess, I did admire Bobby's well-intentioned efforts.

Bobby also gave his best efforts at bottle feeding and spoon feeding Brad. After spoon feeding episodes in the high-chair, a great mess would be left behind; sometimes I could not tell who had made the bigger mess. Anyway, the end result was a fun time for both of them and the development of a strong, loving bond. Playtime consisted of a lot of wrestling mixed with affection. They both loved this type of interaction. Other kinds of play activities for them included basketball, football, swimming, reading, watching movies, video games and bike riding.

How does a blind man play basketball? Well, I guess it's that sixth sense that kicks in, and it's something "visual" people just have to see to believe. Bobby holds the free throwing title from the basketball game last week, out of Brad, Jason, René and Benji. I was inside cooking while Brad and the four adults were playing outside. I heard the amazing story from each of them about Bobby's sinking one ball after the other during their competition. As for football, Bobby and Brad play by Bobby's assuming the quarterback position and Brad the receiver. Brad takes off running and then turns and yells, "Daddy!" Bobby then throws the ball by the location of Brad's voice. This is fun for me to watch and fun for them to play. During swimming, Bobby becomes the human diving board. My part is to verbally direct Bobby to a clear, wide and open area. Bobby's part is to hold Brad high in the air, with Brad standing on his shoulders, and then Bobby propels Brad into the air, like a speeding bullet, creating an exciting splash landing into the water. When other children see the fun they are having, Bobby becomes the human diving board for all of them.

When Brad and Bobby are not playing outside, they enjoy watching television and playing video games. While playing video games, Brad will call Bobby into his room to sit with him. Brad then describes what is happening, what he has accomplished and scored. In this instance, seeing is a minor part of the bigger picture — which is the joy of being together.

Bobby truly knows how to live life fully. He will try just about anything whether it involves playing with Brad or pursuing life goals. I have one last story to share, in order to more fully illustrate who Bobby is.

Brad got a new bike for his sixth birthday, and he wanted us to all go bike riding.

Before Brad was born, Bobby and I owned a two-seater bicycle. I would steer in the front, and Bobby would do most of the pedal work in the back. However, we gave the two-seater bike away several years ago when we moved. So, at the time of Brad's request, all we had were regular bikes, and we loaded them in the van and went to the State Farm parking lot in Monroe. State Farm has a very large parking lot with lots of evenly spaced light poles. This time, during the family bike ride, Bobby did the pedaling and the steering! I rode on the front handlebars and gave verbal instructions, and Brad rode on the back, in a child's seat. We held on for a thrilling ride as Bobby rode us on around, weaving in and out of light poles with us screaming and laughing.

We also switched riding positions because Brad wanted to get the thrill of riding in the front. As Bobby rode Brad, I ran beside them shouting directions. This was a bike ride like none other, with a blind man in the driver's seat and me giving instructions. Added to that was the fact that I kept confusing my left from my right.

We have all learned through Bobby's blindness that there is no one right way to accomplish various tasks. With creative thinking and a healthy amount of risk taking, many things can be accomplished.

In closing, I'll tell you a little about the work God has called me to do. As I mentioned earlier, when Bobby and I first met, I was a practicing dietitian/nutritionist. Today, I also practice mental health counseling. Many times, Bobby joked with me and others that God had sent him a nutritionist/counselor to be his wife, because he had been shot in the head, had brain damage, and had an eating disorder. Could it be coincidental that we got married and that our strengths and weaknesses compliment one another? I think not. God had a hand in this!

I believe that we are all members of the Body of Christ and are all called on to love and serve those with whom we come in contact. It is my hope and prayer that this book will be a blessing to you. Each night I pray with my son and say the blessing from the Book of Numbers(6:24-26). I'd also like to say it to you: "May the Lord bless you and keep you; may His face shine upon you and be gracious to you; and may He turn His face toward you and give you peace." Love, Janie.

I received a call one day from Sgt. Al Edwards of

the Fredericksburg, Virginia, Police Department. Al told me that he had heard me speak at one of the conferences in New Orleans, and he wanted me to come to Virginia to do a lecture for their department and academy. I told him that would be fine. He then told me that they were also going to try and get me in to meet President Reagan. I was astounded!

"You're joking, I'm going to get to meet the President of the United States," I said.

He told me that he wasn't sure, but they were trying to set it up, so when I came, I was to make sure I brought a Louisiana State Police belt buckle, because President Reagan collected law enforcement memorabilia.

I went by the LSTA office and told them I was going to Washington, D.C., to meet President Reagan. They all laughed.

"You've got to be joking," they said.

"No," I replied. "I really think I am going to meet him."

I told them that he collected law enforcement memorabilia, and I needed a State Police belt buckle to give him. They gladly gave me a buckle and I went home. They didn't really believe that I would actually get to meet President Reagan. But I did; I really did.

Steve Barrett, Janie and I caught a plane and flew to Virginia. Al met us at the airport. Steve and I were both scheduled to do a presentation at the academy. Steve was a good lecturer on police training, but he was also a Cajun humorist. Everyone loved him!

Al told us that he would come pick us up at the hotel the next day, and we would go into Washington, D.C., to meet President Reagan. We arrived in D.C. about mid morning. We met some of the police officers there and went to meet Major Carl Homburg. Major Homburg was in charge of air security for the President.

They took us to the airport and put Janie and I in the helicopter, Air 1. We flew around all of the DC area looking at all the monuments and the White House.

Janie began to cry when she said, "Bobby, I wish you could see this. It's absolutely incredible."

When the helicopter landed, we went to the White House. I couldn't believe it, I was 34 years old and for the first time, I was going to the White House, the Capitol of our country, to meet the President of the United States, and I couldn't even see it.

The secret service agents met us out front and escorted us inside. When they brought us in, they took us to a small room right inside the door and began running scanners all over us to make sure we weren't carrying any weapons. We had to fill out a lot of forms and provide our identifications.

We then proceeded down a long hallway. It seemed like we were walking in a canyon, because the walls were so wide and the ceiling was so high. It was incredible, absolutely unbelievable! Next, we walked down to the doors that led to the rose garden. As we were standing just inside the doors, a young lady walked up to me, stuck out her hand and introduced herself.

"Mr. Smith, I'm the President's assistant, and he will be down in just a minute to meet you and your wife," she said.

I would like to believe that I am a pretty cool headed guy and I don't stress out easily. I had played a lot of roles before while I was working undercover as a police officer and had learned to keep my cool. But this was different; it was really difficult. Within just a minute, I heard people walking down the hall. I knew it was the President and his entourage. They started walking toward us and cameras started snapping. Wow, they're taking pictures, not one or two, but what seemed to be hundreds.

As the President walked up to Janie and I, I reached out my hand and tried to think of something to say. Nothing came to mind. He walked right past me and hugged Janie.

He turned to me and said, "I always hug the pretty women first."

Then he shook my hand. His hand was larger than mine and he had a strong but caring handshake. Then President Reagan said, "Trooper Smith, I understand you were involved in a shooting and lost your sight. I was involved in a shooting once myself. I've been there, and it's not very pleasant."

I agreed with him. He went on to say what great respect he had for law enforcement. He said that when he was shot, the law enforcement officers were there to lay their lives down for him, and also for the public. I began thinking, there must be a flag flying somewhere in the background, because man, this was patriotic! I then reached in my pocket and pulled out the brass belt buckle that the Trooper Association had given me. As I handed it to the President, I told him that I had heard that he collected law enforcement memorabilia. He was delighted! He was just like a little kid with a new toy.

He laughed out loud, "I guess the word's got around that I collect belt buckles from police officers."

He told me when I went back home, to tell everyone thank you, and that when he went to the ranch that weekend, he was going to wear it. I couldn't stop smiling.

We talked for a few minutes more, and he asked me how long we were going to be in town. I told him that we would be there several days.

"How would you two like to come back this evening to see everything in the White House? " he asked.

I was totally flabbergasted and said, "That would be great!"

He turned to the secret service agent next to me and told him that when we came back, he was to show us anything we wanted to see. He said that we could go anywhere we wanted to go, and that there would be no restrictions. He then told him to take me to the Oval Office first.

We went through every room in the White House, the President's library, the War Room, the Press Room, and the Communication Room. It was incredible! They explained everything to us as we went. Then we went to the Oval Office and I stood behind President Reagan's desk. The secret service agent said, "Go ahead, take a seat in the President's chair." I told him that I couldn't. As I stood there, I touched his desk and chair. It was unbelievable! I couldn't bring myself to sit in his chair, because that chair was reserved for the President, and him only. I would never violate that honor.

When we returned home, I knew it was now time for me to start deciding what I was going to do with my professional career. What could I do? I was always interested in psychology and counseling, and after what I had been through, I felt that I would be pretty good at it. So, I enrolled in school and started taking some courses in Counseling Psychology. I was really enjoying learning how to counsel and how to deal with my own issues.

The State Trooper's Association hired me to do peer counseling for the troopers. Things were looking up, and maybe I could still be productive in the law enforcement capacity. It really felt great to be a part of it again.

Janie and I had been married almost a year. I was 36

and she was 29. We began talking about starting a family, and shortly thereafter, Janie came in one day and told me that she was pregnant. This was a happy time for us! We both wanted another child. Janie had never had any children, but I had my daughter, Kim, from a previous marriage. Everything was going great for us, and her pregnancy was going well. I had started my classes at Louisiana College and was still continuing to travel around the country lecturing on Officer Survival.

One day, I made an appointment with the department head of psychology at the university, and told him that I wanted to talk with him in reference to seeing what I needed to do to enter graduate school. He told me to come by and see him, and that he looked forward to meeting me. I didn't tell him I was blind.

The next day, I got a friend of mine to take me to his office. My friend stopped at the door, and I walked in his office with my cane in my hand. I could sense by his reaction that he was a little shocked to see me there with my cane and dark sunglasses. I could only imagine what this man was thinking. I reached out my hand to shake his hand, but I was too far away from him, because he was still standing behind his desk.

He walked around his desk, shook my hand and told me to have a seat. He made an attempt to help me to a chair but was very awkward about it. I found the chair on my own and had a seat.

I began telling him about how I was shot as a Louisiana State Trooper and that I had been traveling all over the country speaking. I went on to tell him that I was currently working for the State Police as a peer counselor and that I wanted to get my Master's degree in Counseling Psychology. He told me how difficult it would be. First of all, I would have to pass the Graduate's Records Exam (GRE), which he said was very difficult for a sighted person, much less someone who was blind. If I got through that, I would then have to go before the Interview Board. He told me that the board would have to be assured that if they accepted me, I would be able to handle the load. I would have to carry at least nine hours, do term papers in each class, and present them to the class.

"Are you prepared to do that?" he asked. I told him that I would do whatever I had to do to get through graduate school. This was something I really wanted to do.

He did everything he could to try and talk me out of entering his graduate program. He ended our conversation by telling me that he didn't think it was a very good idea for me to even try to enter the program. He didn't see how I could do all the studying, prepare all the papers, much less present them to the class without any written notes to guide me. He then went on to tell me that he thought I should look into another field of study, maybe one that wasn't quite so hard; one that would be easier for me under my circumstances.

I was furious! It reminded me of the day that I had my meeting with Colonel Wiley McCormick. I felt the rage and anger boiling. Not again. Not another person in a position of authority and power who would make the decision for me, of whether or not I would be successful in life, based on their ignorant perceptions of blindness! I was infuriated!

I went by the registrar's office and picked up the paperwork to set up the date to take the GRE. The test was scheduled for several weeks later. When I took the test, I did extremely well. I wanted to send this particular professor a copy of my test results, so I could rub it in his face. I wanted to make him eat his words for insinuating that I was too stupid to pass a test of this magnitude because I was blind. I knew this wasn't the right thing to do, so I didn't.

CHAPTER 34
MOVING BACK TO MONROE

It had been almost three years since living in Monroe, and now I was moving back. There was still some anxiety there. Would it be the same? Would those dragons still be there, licking their chops, as they anticipated my return? I was hoping that I had worked through most of those things, and I felt that I had. I was looking forward to moving back and being able to spend more time with Kim and my old friends, the police family in Monroe. In all, I was excited about this move.

I applied for graduate school at Northeast Louisiana University (NLU) in Monroe and had been accepted. I changed my major from Counseling Psychology to Exercise Physiology. As an exercise enthusiast, I had always tried to stay in excellent physical condition and had helped many other police officers do the same. I decided that this would be a good field, so I could stay involved with law enforcement in the exercise capacity. I thought I would develop exercise programs for police departments.

Janie and I moved to West Monroe and lived in a small rental house until we got the chance to build one. I went to work for the West Monroe Police Department and started developing an exercise program for Chief Larry LaBorde's department.

I got a call from Dr. Billy Daniels, the Department Head of the Health and Human Performance at NLU. He informed me that I had been accepted into the graduate program and also offered me a job as a graduate assistant working in the Exercise Physiology Lab. He then advised me of a mandatory graduate assistantship meeting the following morning.

I had been going to school as a blind person for the last year and a half, but this was different. It was like going from the minor league to the major leagues. I was in graduate school now, and there were strenuous requirements. I knew there would be a lot of term papers, and studying would be exhausting. I had some apprehension and anxiety.

My dad had told me that if I wanted to be successful, and if I wanted to complete an assignment that I had started, I needed to put myself in a position where I couldn't turn back. It was kind of like jumping off a cliff. Once you jump, there's no turning back. I made that jump when I entered graduate school; I had no choice but to finish.

We met in the conference room of the performance lab. I sat next to a lady I had never met before. Dr. Daniels began going around the room introducing everyone. There were probably fifteen or twenty of us. Dr. Daniels introduced me but failed to mention that I was blind. Then he went to Stephanie Wells, the young lady sitting to my left. She was from Arkansas and had played college basketball and was now going to NLU to work on her graduate degree in Exercise Physiology.

When the meeting was over, I introduced myself to Stephanie and asked her if she would help me with my reading some time. I could sense that she was looking at me very puzzled. I'm sure she thought, "You're in graduate school and you don't know how to read?" I told her that I was blind, but she didn't believe me at first. We became very good friends. She helped me with my library assignments, my term papers, and we studied together almost daily.

A few months later Stephanie came to work at the

police department with me, as my assistant, helping me run the exercise program for the West Monroe Police Department. We had a lot of fun, and I got in what was probably the best shape I had ever been in my life. She was a marathoner, a triathelete, and she knew how to get you in shape.

One thing was sure, graduate school was hard. I went to class everyday with my tape recorder. I recorded the class then went home and listened to the recorded lecture once more. This time I took notes on another tape recorder. Day after day I repeated this routine. At the end of the week, I reviewed every class and put it on an additional tape, and that was the tape that I would study from for the tests. I studied for four to six hours every day. I did extremely well in all the classes that I took, not because I was smarter than all the students, but because I was more determined. I had something to prove. I'm not sure if my desire was for myself or for those people who thought I couldn't do it — probably both. But, I had to succeed; I felt I had no choice.

VISIONS OF COURAGE

CHAPTER 35
RETIRING F-18

I was sitting at my desk early one morning, when Lt. Charlie Heard, the executive officer from the Louisiana State Police, Troop F office called. He told me that he thought he had some good news for me. He went on to say that he knew I was aware that a request had been made by the troopers to retire my plate, but thus far, the request had been denied. He said that now they were going up the chain of command, to Major Rutt Whittington at Region III in Alexandria. He thought that once we put the ball in Major Whittington's court, that he would go ahead and approve the request.

"I can't promise you anything, Bobby, but it would mean a lot to us, and I know it would mean a lot to you also," Lt. Heard said.

I could feel the emotions of the impact of what he had just told me. First it started in my chest, then it went to my throat, and I was fighting back tears. They were tears of sadness and happiness. Oh, how I longed to put that uniform on one more time and call the troop and say, "F-18's 10-8, in service." But, I was also happy because I knew it was my number. That was my identification, F-18 was Trooper Bobby Smith. Now they were going to retire my number. They were going to take my plate, F-18, along with my picture, put it in a shadow box and place it in the foyer of the troop as a tribute to me. All I could say without crying was, "Thank-you, Lieutenant." He picked up on the emotion in my voice and told me that he would talk with me later.

As I sat there at my desk, the tears rolled down my

face. Now I was angry. The Colonel and the State Police administration had done everything they could to make sure that I just went away, but the troopers themselves had never given up on me. The troopers were the ones that had made the request through the State Police rank to retire my plate. This was something that they wanted to do for me, but also something they needed to do for themselves.

A couple of weeks passed, and I was sitting at my desk when Chief LaBorde came by for a visit. He asked what I was doing and I told him not much. He invited me to go to lunch, and I agreed. He handed me my jacket and I put it on, unaware that there were police officers lined up down the walls of the hallway. We walked down the hallway toward the conference room. I knew this wasn't the way out so I asked him what we were doing. He told me that he had to get something off the briefing board. I felt that something was going on, but I wasn't sure of what it could have been. We never wore our coats when we went to lunch. What was going on?

Jackie Coleman was there. He walked up to me, hugged my neck and told me that he loved me. At that moment, the room erupted into a round of applause. Major Rutt Whittington walked up to me and shook my hand. He then handed me a shadow box and told me that this was for me. He went on to tell me that inside that shadow box was my State Police plate, F-18, my ACE plate, my State Police picture, and the scripture Isaiah 40:31. It read: *"For those that wait upon the Lord shall renew their strength, they shall mount up with wings as eagles, you shall run and not be weary, you shall walk and not faint."*

The major said, "Bobby, this shadow box is for you to place in your home, and the other one will be placed in the front foyer of Troop F in Monroe, to remind all of us of the job that you did as a state trooper and also what you have done since your shooting. We are very proud of you and we love you."

The tears were unashamedly rolling down my face, and through the tears in a low voice I said, "Thank you so much."

Yet, it seemed as if too many good things were now taking place in my life. I had been accepted into graduate school, with a graduate assistantship, was hired at the police department to develop their physical fitness program, and now, finally, my State Police plate was being retired. Man, could anything better happen? But something better did happen. My son was born February 12, 1990.

Kim was fifteen, and now I had a son, Brad Elliott Smith. Up to this point, I only thought that I had accomplished some monumental goals in my life. I only thought I had had some serious challenges. It was extremely challenging trying to be a blind dad while helping Janie at home. But, just like everything else, I learned to adjust.

VISIONS OF COURAGE

CHAPTER 36
"YOU CAN'T JUST TAKE OFF THE BLINDFOLD"
Carol Mathus,
Personal Assistant

When I first met Bobby, I was going through a very difficult time in my life. A friend of mine was working with him as his assistant, and she had told me about him. One day she and I had made lunch plans, so I went to get her. That was the day I met Bobby. I liked him because he was full of bull, a lot like me. Bobby and I chatted for a while, just small talk, until my friend finished up her work and was ready to go to lunch. He asked where we were going. I told him and invited him to go, but he declined, stating that he already had plans. I gave him a hard time about not wanting to go, so in his defense, he agreed to go to lunch another day.

The next week I called Bobby to see if he wanted to go to lunch, and he agreed but told me that I would have to pick him up because he didn't drive very well during the day. So, the next day, I picked him up for lunch. As we drove to the restaurant, we began to talk. It was like I had known him my whole life. At this time, I desperately needed someone to talk to because I was going through a divorce. I needed to talk with someone who understood what I was feeling, and Bobby was that person. He had gone through a divorce, and he knew the pain that I was suffering. I felt that God placed Bobby in my life for a special reason, and I was glad.

As we arrived at the restaurant, there was a sense of comfort, but I was also very cautious of my movements around

251

him. I didn't want to run him into anything, so I was trying to be very alert. We were seated and began to eat lunch. While we were eating, the waitress came and refilled Bobby's water glass, but she didn't put it back in the same spot. He reached for his glass, but I had seen it coming. At that time, I had a four year old daughter and I was always trying to avoid as many spills as possible. I reached out and placed my hand on the top of his glass, just in time, to keep it from turning over. We both laughed.

As time went on, it seemed like everytime I called to talk to my friend, he would pick up the phone. God was not giving up, He was going to keep placing Bobby in my life. Even during this horrible time of my life, Bobby made me laugh, something I hadn't done in a long time.

I had always been very athletic growing up and enjoyed working out. And so did he. We began working out together at the West Monroe Police gym where he worked. We would talk as we worked out. At first, he would talk and I would listen, and as time went by, I finally began to talk to him and he would really listen to me. I had finally found someone I could talk to. It was so comforting to be with him and share my feelings. We became good friends as time progressed.

At that time, I was working a part time job and had some free time. Bobby would call when he needed a ride or if he needed me to do something for him, and I would do whatever he needed. He made me feel needed again. I remember feeling that I must have been an important person because he needed my help. Looking back today, I know that he knew the pain and sorrow I was feeling and probably asked for my help more to help me, than to help himself. But that's what made this man, my new friend, so different from other people. He saw the needs in others, and cared enough to try to make a difference.

I began taking him to his speaking engagements and listening to his presentations. He always told the audience to go home and put on a blindfold, so they could better understand what his world was like. So one day after I dropped him off at his house, I went home. I had watched him maneuver through his split level home, and had watched him go up and down those stairs just like anyone else. I decided to try out that dark world.

I lived in a two-story townhouse. I put on a blindfold and carefully made my way to the stairs. I had watched him maneuver steps so many times, and he made it seem so easy, so this was where I decided to start. I got to the bottom of the stairs and scary thoughts began to run through my head. How would I know how many steps there were? What if my daughter had left a toy on the stairs? Would I really be able to make it? As I took that first step I remember thinking, this isn't going to be so bad. Surely I can do this.

I went up the first section of steps and then turned to start up the next. Would I ever make it? It seemed like forever had passed and being scared of the dark didn't help either! I hadn't checked upstairs when I first got home. What if someone had broken in and was waiting upstairs? I took the next four steps to the top and as soon as my foot hit, I snatched my blindfold off. My heart was racing like crazy! That is when I realized, only for those few moments, what my friend goes through 24 hours a day. All I had to do was reach up and take my blindfold off. His blindfold never comes off.

Shortly thereafter, Bobby began to need more assistance because his assistant had moved to another position at the department. I left the job I was at and started helping him. I have been with him for the last five and a half years, as both his assistant and friend, and fashion designer. In the evenings, when we got home from work, I laid out his clothes for the next day to try and help before I went home. I helped him buy his clothes because he was very particular about the way he looked. At times I got so frustrated with him when I was trying to get him to update his wardrobe. We had many arguments in department stores over what he was and what he was not going to wear. I felt like a mother fussing with a child about his clothes, and believe me, he was like a child! So, I just started buying him clothes when I would go shopping and bring them home for him to wear.

Sometimes when I picked Bobby up in the mornings, he had on a dark blue sock with a black one. We would have to go back in to change his socks and try to find some that matched. This always frustrated him because of his obsession with his appearance. He always referred to the blind students in Ruston and how they dressed. He would not accept that. He had to be matched and looking good when he went out. He would always say that he may have been blind, but he didn't have to look it. I thought it was because looking blind would mean that he had accepted it, and he wouldn't do that. I always told him that he had better be nice to me because I could really make him look bad by mismatching his clothes.

Well, we have been together a long time now, and he is my best friend. We have been through some sorrows and pain but also joy and gladness. I have grown to love this man just like one of my family. During the time that we have known each other, my life has changed tremendously and I owe it all to God. If it hadn't been for God placing Bobby Smith in my life five and a half years ago, I don't know where I would be today. I thank God for placing such a special friend in my life. People say that you only have a few true friends in your lifetime, and I can truly say that he has been that kind of friend to me.

CHAPTER 37
THE GRADUATION

I finally made it through graduate school, praise God! I didn't think that day would ever arrive. The long hours of studying, the term papers I had to present in every class, every semester, were finally over. I had had enough of the classrooms. But I still had one final hurdle, the oral interview with all of my professors, and the comprehensive exam of all the courses that I had taken for the last year and a half. I had studied for weeks and was still worried if I would know the information well enough.

I studied a while and prayed a while. Then I would study some more and pray some more. I guess both must have worked, because I passed my comprehensive exam. Thank God it was over!

I called Kim and told her that I had passed my comprehensive exam and that I would graduate. I told her that I needed her to do me a favor.

She replied, "What, Dad? I'll do anything for you."

I told her that I would like for her to walk me across the stage to get my diploma.

"Oh, Dad, you want me to do that?"

I told her that I couldn't think of anyone that I would rather have walk me across that stage.

"Oh Dad, I would be delighted!"

That greatly anticipated graduation day finally came. As the graduates began arriving, we began lining up in alphabetical order and started taking our seats for the ceremony. The university president, Dr. Dwight Vines, got up, introduced the special speaker for the day, and welcomed the guests. President Vines then began recognizing all of the candidates who had received their Ph.D.'s. Then he went on to the ones who had received their Specialist Degrees, and after that, the ones who had received Masters Degrees. He went down the list in alphabetical order. One at a time he called their names. When Dr. Vines called out my name, Bobby Smith, he paused. I noticed that he hadn't paused on any of the other graduates.

Dr. Vines had been the president of the university for years, and we had known each other for fifteen of those years. And now here I was, receiving a second diploma from him.

After he announced my name, he began telling everyone my story, and they listened very intently. When he finished, he went on to announce all the other graduates. We then listened to the guest speaker, and then it was time to receive our diplomas.

Once again Dr. Vines began announcing the names of those who had received their Ph.D. Degrees and on down to the ones receiving Masters Degrees. Then he got to my name.

"Our next graduate to receive a diploma for a Masters Degree in Education, Bobby Smith," he announced.

I rose to my feet, escorted by Kim, started walking down the aisle and up onto the stage. We had only taken a few steps when the whole coliseum erupted into applause. I was fighting back those tears once again, but this time it was tears of joy and happiness. I had finally made it! I had been quite successful, for I graduated with honors. What more could I ask for?

My daughter leaned over, hugged me, and kissed me on the cheek. As she hugged me, she said, "Dad, they are giving you a standing ovation!"

CHAPTER 38
I WAS SITTING AT MY DESK

I had spoken hundreds of times in my speaking career, but this was different. There were butterflies in my stomach. I was nervous to some extent. There was some anticipation of how we would be received by all these people. People were there for one reason; how much we could make in their stocks this quarter. The bottom line was money. I spoke in a large auditorium with rows and rows of seats. In front of the auditorium, there was a podium with chairs to the right. Sitting in each chair was a board member from Time Warner. At the head table was the CEO, Jim LaVene. Mr. LaVene took the, microphone and addressed the stockholders of Time Warner.

"Before we commence with our business meeting, we have a special guest to go over our position on one of the projects that Time Warner has produced and distributed. It seemed as though there is some opposition to the project called Cop Killer by the rap artist Ice T. At this time, we will allow him to make a presentation on our position on this album."

As the speaker was recognized, he walked to the podium in the center of the auditorium. "Members of the media, I am here representing police officers around the country. Some cannot be here today, because they have been slain in the line of duty. Some of those were assassinated, assassinated by people who wanted to tear down the fence between crime and you, the citizens of this country. Today, I would like you to hear personal stories from police officers around the country who have been shot in the line of duty by such people. It is our hope here today that you would hear these officers and vote to stop the production and distribution of the album, Cop Killer.

One by one, police officers walked to the podium, some white, some black, some female, some male. Each one told their story of how they had been personally affected by being shot themselves, losing a partner, sometimes losing husbands and some losing wives in the line of duty while being a police officer. Each story was heart wrenching. As I sat there waiting my turn, I could hear the sniffling and the coughing, the sounds I associate with people holding back their emotions. There were lots and lots of emotions being held back in that room. Occasionally, a stockholder would walk to a side podium and complain about us even being there, but a majority of jeers among the stockholders would put them in their place. It became painfully obvious to the board of directors at Time Warner that the stockholders were also in opposition to the rapster's album, Cop Killer. It was becoming obvious that what was happening here today was a conflict in making money and what was morally correct. The scale was leaning to what was morally right and moving this album off the shelves. A quiet fell among the crowd as I heard someone make their way to the podium.

"Mr. Chairman," a voice rang out, slow, articulate, forceful. "If I may be recognized."

I leaned over to Chief LaBorde. "Is that Charlton Heston?"

"Yes, it is."

It was as if Moses himself was standing at the Red Sea trying to part it and he was facing the Egyptian army. It was hard to see him as Charlton Heston. To me, he was Moses, and he was there to right a wrong and set the captives free. Once again, he stated, "Mr. Chairman, may I be recognized?" But there was no response. He stood there stoic, looking straight ahead, with his hands folded in front of him.

"Mr. Heston, please have a seat. You have not been recognized."

But he stood there, motionless, looking straight ahead. "Mr. Chairman, may I be recognized?" Again he was told to sit down, and he sat there looking straight ahead.

Wow, this was just like a movie. A stockholder stood up and said, "Let Mr. Heston speak. He's a stockholder. He has a right to speak, so recognize him to speak."

"Mr. Heston, please sit down. You have not been recognized."

"Mr. Chairman, Mr. Heston has every right to speak and please allow him to be recognized so he can speak," a female stockholder said.

The tension was mounting in the room. I kept thinking to myself, "There must be a movie projector running somewhere." We were in Hollywood, but reality soon came back through the sniffs and the coughs of the people standing up against a gangster rapper who was advocating the killing of the front lines of defense of this country: the police officers. Mr. Heston was finally recognized, and he began to speak, saying that cops were appointed and ordained by God to be the defenders and centurions, to protect and serve the citizens of the United States of America. Time Warner had allowed gangster rappers to produce an album that advocated the killing of our front lines, and we, as a people, were outraged. This album needed to be pulled from the shelves, and production and distribution stopped.

The auditorium rose to its feet in applause of what Mr. Heston said. We needed to protect our cops. We needed to stand up as a country and protect them. As graciously as he appeared, Mr. Heston turned and walked from the podium.

Once again, a moment of silence fell across the air. "Our next speaker will be Bobby Smith. In 1986, Trooper Smith was involved in a shooting with a suspect who hated police officers, and in an attempt to take Trooper Smith's life, he shot Trooper Smith in the face, totally blinding him. He has had to live in a world of darkness as a result of someone's hatred toward police officers. Please welcome Trooper Bobby Smith."

I felt the butterflies in my stomach as he announced my name. Chief LaBorde and I stood and walked to the podium. He stood there much like a bodyguard would do for a rock star, but this was no visage. There was no dramatic ending to this play. This was reality.

As I began to speak, I could feel the emotions begin to tear at my chest. I fought back the tears. I fought back the emotions in my voice, and I hoped I wouldn't start crying. The loss of my eyesight is important to me. I told how I would never be able to see my beautiful daughter's smile ever again. I would never be able to pitch with her in the front yard or watch her cheer or ride her horse. I would never get to see her mature into a young woman. I would never be able to see Brad's face. My emotions were taking over. I didn't have anything else to say before I broke down in sobs. I turned to my left, and I faced the executive table. I pointed my finger at myself, "Mr. LaVene, it is reasonably obvious to me that you have never been shot in the face. It is also extremely obvious that you are totally blind."

I turned and began walking back to my seat. Chief LaBorde grabbed my arm and escorted me, and I sat there with tears running down my face from the emotions of losing my sight and the thoughts that I would never see my beautiful children ever again. It broke my heart at the audacity of money-hungry people, who thought more about making money than saving the lives of the cops of this country. I felt outraged. I sat there with tears on my face when Chief LaBorde leaned over, "Bobby, you got their attention. Jim LaVene has got his head in his hands and is looking at the floor. His wife is sitting right next to him and has tears running down her face. Bobby, you've done it."

The presentation was over, and we, as their special guests, were asked to leave so they could continue their meeting. We walked outside, and all the major networks were there interviewing Charlton Heston, myself and other police officers who had spoken on our behalf. There were also advocates there who supported Mr. Ice T. In a sudden panic, people were running and shouting everywhere. The cameramen were shouting. There went Mr. Ice T himself, driving through the parking lot of the Beverly Hills Hilton where we were gathered. As Mr. Ice T pulled through in his convertible Mercedes, he lifted up his hand and made an obscene gesture. He sped out of the parking lot and exited without ever stopping.

We returned to Monroe. A couple of weeks later we saw that Time Warner stockholders had voted to stop the production and distribution of Cop Killer and removed all remaining albums from the shelf.

I've never been much of a fence rider. It's usually pretty obvious what side of the fence that I am on. I had been asked several times to appear on talk shows and talk about toxic substances, gun control, freedom of speech and religion and separation of church and state. I don't want to say that I am always right or that my opinion is always correct, but that is what is good about America. Each one of us has our own voice. As a result of my philosophy and mentality as an American, I felt that we needed people in politics who would stand up and say the right thing, and do it.

It was spring of 1995, and the sheriff of Ouachita Parish had announced that he would not seek reelection. People began to throw their names in the hat. Why not me? I decided. There were mixed emotions about my campaign. My friends were not very supportive. Some were constructive in their criticism.

"Bobby, you are blind. No one would elect a blind man. They still have that Mayberry mentality that the sheriff has to be out following all the crime. They don't understand it is an administrative position. You've got an uphill climb."

I was used to uphill. I had overcome a lot in the last nine years. It couldn't be worse in a political campaign. Or so I thought. I got a great lesson in politics. It's almost a win at all cost philosophy. It is extremely draining on candidates and their families. Lies and deceptions are spread on each candidate by each candidate, which didn't make much sense to me. If you've got to lie about each other as a candidate, then you would also lie in office. Oh well, welcome to America. When it was all said and done, I did fairly well but not well enough. I came in third out of six. The front runner was Richard Fewell, who was the chief deputy at that time. The man that came in a strong second was Chuck Cook, a former police officer who was now a prosecuting attorney. Chuck came to solicit my support. I ran for sheriff because I felt like we needed a positive, progressive change. It didn't work out that way, but I felt like Chuck Cook, who's platform for change was similar to mine, would do the better job. I publicly endorsed him. In the runoff election, Mr. Cook won. In his victory speech, he stated, "I couldn't have won without my endorsement." Now don't take me wrong.

THE BOBBY SMITH STORY

I am not that arrogant. I was only just a part to help him get elected, but that acknowledgment from him towards me would become bittersweet.

Two months later, Mr. Cook, after assuring me about some things he would and would not do, offered me a job to go to work in his personnel and training division. I accepted. Chuck has a typical police personality: authoritative, controlling, loves his power and is narcissistic. It only took a couple of months for me to realize that I had made a mistake endorsing him for sheriff. I had put my reputation, my name and my integrity on the line. Now I doubted myself on whether I had done the right thing. I felt that I had been lied to by him. It turned out, I had been lied to. The things he promised not to do, he did do. The things he promised to do, he didn't do. In the first supervisor's meeting in the second month of his office, it became crystal clear that I had made a horrible mistake in endorsing him for sheriff.

As he stood at the podium, he said, "You people need to understand one thing: I was the one elected sheriff, not you. You work for me. I don't work for you, and I will respect you after you respect me first."

I felt the chills run down the back of my neck. What had I done? It didn't take long for controversies to begin to rear their ugly head under his administration. After nine months in office, he was now under investigation by the state police for obstruction of justice and malfeasance in a drug investigation against his stepdaughter, in which it was alleged that he had given information to his stepdaughter, and that she was being investigated by Metro Narcotics, which was headed by Larry Norris. Norris and I had been personal friends for over twenty-five years.

Cook wanted to know where I stood. He called me to his office and when we were through, it was obvious that I

263

disagreed with his opinion on the investigation and of Larry Norris. Larry Norris was terminated by Cook, and then I became a target of investigation by Sheriff Cook.

For the next several months, I would be the target of an internal affairs investigation. He tried to discredit my character and my commitment to being a police officer, because I had sided with Larry Norris.

CHAPTER 39
JUST A PLAIN COTTON DRESS

It was the early morning hours of Sept. 29th, 1997. The phone rang. It was 4:05 a.m. Thoughts began to run through my mind very quickly. As a parent, I was thinking, Has something happened to Kim? Are my parents all right? Has there been a death in my family? I pulled the covers back from the bed and grabbed the phone.

"Hello?"

It was Jackie Bailey, Kim's mom. "Bobby, it's me." She was trying to talk through her tears. My heart sank as the fear of the message ran through my body. "Kim's been involved in a horrible accident, Bobby. They don't know if she is going to make it." I hung the phone up and fell to my knees beside the bed. I prayed, "Please, God, don't let Kim die."

I grabbed the phone and called Troop F. The guys at Troop F had always been there for me. I would surely need them now. I spoke with Trooper Cam Douglas. Everyone was already aware of Kim's accident.

"Bobby, I am enroute to pick you up. I will be there in just a minute."

Cam and I sped to the hospital. Not many words were spoken. Cam is a Christian man. He and I were just praying. In the silence, I began to drift back in time and reminisce about Kim.

It was August 2, 1975, and I was a rookie police man at the Monroe Police Department. I was working on a traffic accident at Stanley Avenue and Desiard Street. The walkie talkie rang at my side. "Headquarters 108."

I grabbed it. "108, go ahead."

"Bobby, are you almost through with that accident? You need to get to the hospital. Jackie is having the baby."

By the time I got to the hospital, Jackie had already had the baby, and they had moved her to a room. There she was, this precious little child. Kimberly Denyce Smith. I could see her in my mind: changing diapers, rocking her to sleep, watching her take her first steps, dropping her off at the babysitter's when Jackie and I had to go to work. Kim would always cry and hold on to my neck. "Daddy, please don't leave. Let me go with you."

I made a lot of mistakes with Kim, and I failed miserably at being her father. It wasn't until I married Janie in 1988 that she made me realize the importance of spending quality time with Kim. But was it too late? Had I been gone too long? Had I been out of her life too many years to come back now and be her dad? Kim was thirteen years old. I remember watching her as she changed from a little girl into a young lady and into a woman. In 1990, Brad was born, and we all moved back to Monroe. Janie was very loving and kind to Kim and accepted her as her own child. Now I was ready to just be a dad. Kim was ready to be a teenager. The next four years of her life would be filled with activities and excitement, but at least I was getting to spend more time with her. I watched her grow into a beautiful young lady. She would enter college, and later, massage therapy school. This four-year period would be a very difficult and emotional time for Kim. She was diagnosed with bi-polar disorder, and she experienced extreme highs and lows. She would also make some wrong choices concerning men in her life, and from mine and her mother's perspective, Kim had fallen into the wrong crowd. Jackie and I had never used drugs or never been around anyone who did, and we never understood why Kim had chosen to do that or chosen to take that road.

On August 2, 1997, Kim's birthday, she and I were eating lunch. We always tried to have Chinese food. We had just gotten back from a family vacation. As we were eating lunch, Kim began to share with me about her past mistakes.

She said, "Dad, I know I have made some mistakes, and I know that I have disappointed you and mom. I want you to know how much I love you. Dad, I am getting my life in order. I am not going to run with those people any more. I want to go back to college and get my degree."

I remember thinking, "Thank God, she is finally getting her head on straight. I am being a dad, and things were going to be good."

As we left the restaurant that day, Kim took me back to my office and gave me a big hug and kiss on the cheek. I was totally unaware that would be the last birthday I would spend with Kim.

Cam and I drove up to the emergency room door of Glenwood Hospital in West Monroe, LA. As we walked through the sliding doors, the attending physician bolted across the room.

"Bobby, Dr. Bailey and Jackie are in the back room. Come with me."

"Doctor, how is Kim?"

"It doesn't look very good. I am so sorry."

I walked into a waiting room. Dr. Bailey and Jackie were there along with Jackie's dad. Jackie walked over to me, and we embraced as tears raced down our face.

"Jackie, how is Kim?"

"I don't think she is going to live, Bobby."

I had been there only a few minutes when Dr. Bermudez came in. He is a neurosurgeon, who had seen me when I got shot. He walked up to us and said, "I am so sorry, but Kim is dead. We couldn't save her. We did all we could, but there was too much damage."

"Could I see her?"

"Sure, you can."

Cam and I walked down the hall into an examining room. Kim was lying there on the gurney. I reached down, and I reached for her hand. Her body was still warm and soft. I held her hand in my hand and began to cry.

"Kim, wake up, it's daddy. I'm here to take you home."

But she wouldn't wake up. I held her hand to my chest as I caressed her long, slender fingers. My little girl was gone.

Jackie and I made the funeral arrangements. I called my brother, Terry, to help. We went to the funeral home and picked out a beautiful casket. It was almost like a nightmare. This is not the way it's supposed to be. You aren't supposed to bury your children, for heaven's sake. They are supposed to bury you. Jackie and I stood there in front of Kim's casket as Jackie described what Kim looked like.

"Bobby, she is so pretty. She's dressed in a plain cotton dress, and is barefooted. She just wanted a plain cotton dress. She always told me that if something ever happened to her to make sure that she was barefooted."

She had told her mom that she had wanted to be able to run through the fields of flowers in heaven and feel the flowers on her feet. Today she was feeling the flowers on her feet.

I returned to work two days after Kim's funeral. Within five minutes of my arrival, my supervisor advised me that the sheriff had called him and told him to transfer my assistant, Carol, to another division: adding insult to a devastating injury. I had had enough. In my opinion, Chuck Cook was an evil, vindictive man, whom we need to continue to pray for.

There was too much water in the glass, and I needed a few days to dump some out. While I was off, I realized I couldn't go back. I couldn't work for him any more. With that stinging realization, I wrote a letter to the media. In my letter, I asked the people of Ouachita Parish to please forgive me for endorsing Chuck Cook, that I had made a horrible mistake. I also stated my displeasure concerning Cook's abuse of power in terminating over forty deputies and firing Larry Norris. I also aired my disappointment in the way he had treated me. I knew the letter would lead to my dismissal, and it did.

I heard a preacher say once that as Christians, we are usually in one of three places: entering a crisis, in the midst of a crisis, or coming out of a crisis. I prayed that I was at least beginning the latter.

VISIONS OF COURAGE

CHAPTER 40
WHERE ANGELS TREAD

The year after Kim's death would be emotionally difficult. I missed her tremendously. Although I didn't spend enough time with Kim, I knew that she was only a phone call away if I needed her. There were times that I forgot she was gone, and I would realize that I couldn't reach her by phone. I was being forced to practice what I preached, to grieve and to mourn. I told myself that it was okay to cry; that it was okay to be angry. Angry at Kim for dying. Angry at God for allowing her to die. And even angry at myself. What could I have done different? What should I have done differently? Periodically, I would go to the grave site, but it only brought back memories of her lying in the casket. It was easier for me to deal with her death by focusing on her life, laughter, outgoing personality and the way she always gave herself in everything she did.

I have heard it said that anything bad that happens in our life can be turned into something positive, and good can be gained from that loss. At this particular time, I wasn't so sure of that. At least, I didn't find anything good for me. But Kim had planted a seed that would blossom across the country. I began sharing the story of Kim's life and death and how we take someone's life for granted. We assume we will always have time to spend with the people we care about. I learned that we only have today. That is all we are guaranteed, and we should live it to the fullest. I began spreading the message to thousands of police officers across the country of the importance of spending quality time with your children every day, setting good examples and teaching them to live by the golden rule: Do unto others as you would have them do unto you.

I had lunch with Kim one afternoon, a month prior to her death. Kim began sharing with me the mistakes she has made in her life. How sorry she was about the grief she had caused her mother and me. "Dad, I am sorry that I have made some mistakes, and I hope you forgive me for those mistakes. But do you know how much I love you and mom? Dad, I know that you haven't always been there for me, and I want you to know that I forgive you for that. I know that you love me. You are only human, Dad. You just made some mistakes. You know what, Dad, you are a much better dad blind than you ever were sighted."

Those words pierced me through my heart. She continued, reaching for my hand. "But it's okay, Dad," she said. "I forgive you, because I know that you can see much better blind than you ever could sighted. I love you."

I don't think there is ever a day that goes by that I do not remember that conversation that I had with Kim. It would be the last. Kim was leap years ahead of me when it came to wisdom, and her life would live on.

Kim, Janie and I had discussed opening up a business, a Christian wellness clinic. It would be a place where people could come with a good family environment, a place where people could come for their mental, physical and emotional health and a place where people could come and be helped. Kim was a massage therapist, and Janie was a licensed professional counselor and a registered dietitian. I was an exercise physiologist and was working on my Ph.D. in counseling psychology.

Kim's death had put a damper on that plan. But the dreams of that business would not go away. Janie and I

would continue to pray about the clinic. We started planning and talking to bankers, attorneys and business advisors.
How in the world could we do this? Neither one of us had
a strong business background, but we had faith in God. We
felt this was what God wanted us to do. But what would we
name it? We had written down several choices, but none felt
right. It was very difficult making plans without Kim. But it
was a way for her to live on.

    I guess we all have our different ways of grieving
and coping with our losses. Mine was through exercise.
When my days got too heavy and all I wanted to do was cry
about Kim, I would go upstairs and jog on the treadmill. I
would run and think about Kim and cry. I plugged in Kim's
favorite CD. As I listened to the songs that reminded me so
much of Kim, but being totally blind, it's easy to escape your
surroundings. It's easy to focus on things that aren't really
real. I would visualize as I would run on the treadmill. Today
I was running on the highway, down the road and around the
curves, and there were trees on both sides. The wind was
blowing. As I rounded the curve, there was someone jog-
ging and they were in front of me. It was a young girl. She
was dressed in running attire. There was something different. There were white wings on her back. I found myself trying to focus through my tear-stained eyes. Slowly, the head
turned around. As the young girl looked back at me with a
large smile on her face, I thought "My God, it's Kim." She
threw me a wave and continued to jog out in front of me. My
mind began to race. An angel running down the road. That's
it. Where Angels Run. No, Where Angels Tread. That's it.
Kim had given me the name. Where Angels Tread. She continued to run ahead of me and when I continued and made it
around the curb, she was gone. I turned off the machine and
made it to the stairs. Tears were still running down my face. I

called for Janie. "I've got it! Kim has just given me the name of our business. Where Angels Tread."

I sat down on the floor with Janie. My voice was cracking. My hands were trembling, and tears were running down my face, as I shared the story with Janie. We called our business: Where Angels Tread, the Christian Wellness Clinic. We spent the next year planning, designing, and discussing our moves. Our dream would come true, and Kim would live on. We would find out after opening the doors that it takes more than dreams to make the dream come true. Although we worked very hard and invested everything we had financially, we were forced to close the doors. From an earthly perspective, we had taken a great financial loss, but in the process, we had stored up many treasures in heaven. We chose to focus on the positive of the loss of our business, the many lives that had been changed by coming through our doors, like the marriages that had been saved and the lives that Janie had turned around through her Christian counseling, especially the ones that she had led to Christ. How could you put a financial price on that? When God closes a door, he always opens a window, and God had already started opening a window.

CHAPTER 41
BLINDNESS IS A CHOICE

Janie continued her successful practice as a Christian counselor, and I became a lecturer. God had placed many key people in my life after my shooting. I owe my speaking career to Aubrey Futrell, who got me started telling my story and trying to help others deal with their losses. I would find over the years that God would interject additional people in my life, key people who would help me continue my race.

I was at the State Police Region Three Headquarters in Alexandria, LA, one afternoon talking to Sgt. Steve Barrett, a Louisiana state trooper. I was sharing with him how God always seemed to put key people in my life along the way.

Steve told me, "Bobby, your life is like a relay race. God is handing the baton to different people to run a portion of the race with you, and then pass the baton off to someone else."

I had seen this happen time after time. The baton would be passed to different people as God interjected people in my life. Each runner would get me closer and closer to what God's ultimate goal was.

I was speaking in Columbus, Ohio, at a national drug conference. A friend of mine, a retired lieutenant from the highway patrol, called me over. "Bobby, this is Heidi Marshall, the colonel's daughter."

Heidi was a state police sergeant assigned to the training division. Being a police trainer, Heidi was a superior athlete. She worked out on a regular basis and ran mara-

275

thons. Little did she known, she was being handed the baton and asked to run a leg of the race that would put me closer to one of my goals, earning my Ph. D. The one thing I lacked in getting my doctorate was someone to help me in research and help me write my papers. I needed someone who had the knowledge of law enforcement, but who also had the intellect to write. Heidi had earned a full athletic scholarship to one of the local universities in Ohio earned a degree in religion and an MBA. Over the next nine months, she would work extremely hard to help me achieve my goal, and in the process, become a very dear friend. On November 15, 2000, I received my Ph.D. in counseling/psychology. I would joke with her that the diploma should read "Heidi Ann Marshall" and not "Bobby E. Smith." There is probably more truth than fallacy to that statement.

EPILOGUE

What is my ultimate mission? What am I supposed to be doing with my life? I have been speaking for almost two decades, and my simple prayer has always been just to help someone. I want to be a servant. I want to encourage people along this journey.

It is now 2008. Janie, Brad and I just moved back to Louisiana after living in Missouri for five years. It's good to be back home with family and friends. Brad finished loading up his MDX and headed off to Lafayette, Louisiana where he is starting his freshman year at the University of Louisiana.

On August 8th I was re-commissioned as a Louisiana State Trooper by our new Superintendent of the Louisiana State Police, Col. Michael D. Edmonson. I will be teaching in the Louisiana State Police Training Academy and working with the State Police Peer Support Program. It's good to be back home here as well.

I continue to work Janie to near exhaustion as we revise and reprint my second book, *The Will to Survive* and finish the final editing on my third book, *What's in Your Heart Comes Out Your Mouth*, which will be released this fall. We have several more books on the drawing board. The one we decided to write and publish next is tentatively titled *And the Rain Fell on the Flower*, a book about coping with grief and loss.

In 2001 Janie and I formed The Forte Foundation (Foundation for Officers Recovering from Traumatic Events), a not for profit 501C3 corporation. In 2008 Forte partnered with Daphne Levenson who heads up GSRCPI, Gulf States Regional Center for Public Safety Innovations (www.gsrcpi.org), which is located in Hammond, Louisiana. We will provide counseling and training for police officers and their agencies.

God bless you as you pursue your mission and journey in life. Always remember to Keep the Vision!

-Bobby

Visions of Courage
The Bobby Smith Story

Also Available in Paperback:
The Will To Survive: A Mental and Emotional Guide for Law Enforcement Professionals $20.00
See our other products at www.visionsofcourage.com

For speaking availability and other resources by Bobby Smith, Ph.D. see www.visionsofcourage.com or email at bobbysmith@visionsofcourage.com

(417) 887-1142
(318) 240-8209

BOBBY'S PHILOSOPHY OF LIFE

Don't <u>EVER</u> give up!